THE ROAD TO WHITNEY
Two Schmucks Challenge Themselves and the Wilderness

By Cameron Williams and James Johnson

Copyright © 2018 by Cameron Williams

All rights reserved.

No parts of this book may be reproduced in any form or by any electronic or mechanical means, including information storage and retrieval systems, without written permission from the author except for the use of brief quotations in a book review.

DEDICATION - This book is dedicated to all the average Joe's and Jane's out there that just want to spend some time in nature and challenge themselves (a little), push their limits (a little) and enjoy their times outdoors (a lot).

Top of the World

California Highway 395 to Whitney Portal via Lone Pine is a mostly straight, flat road; easy to drive; no skill required. However, make sure you have a fork to stick it in your eye to rouse you from the monotony of that lonely and desolate stretch of blacktop. Conversely, if you happen to be approaching Mount Whitney from the west side of the Sierra Nevada, you will not need the fork. You may, however, need a pail, as you will be traversing the mountains via Tioga Road. Tioga Road is located in Yosemite National Park and goes over the Sierra Nevada Mountain Range from West to East (or East to West depending on your direction). The scenery is terrific and ever-changing, as is the direction and elevation of the road, so if you have the slightest compulsion towards motion sickness, you will surely be spending time on the side of the road waiting for nausea or your latest meal to pass (the aforementioned pail will be required if riding with someone who refuses to stop).

I live in Fresno. This industrial-agricultural hamlet boasts more than half-million residents in California's Central Valley and makes for a great staging area for excursions into the three nearby world-class national parks. I could take either route to the town of Lone Pine and the Mount Whitney portal. I could drive into Yosemite, cross the Sierra Nevadas via Tioga Road, watch James throw-up countless times, take 395 south (no ocular utensils required) and arrive in Lone Pine in about five hours. Or, I could take 99 South, cross the Sierra Nevadas through the Tehachapi Pass (safe road for James) then drive North on 395, using more than one fork to stay awake and arrive in Lone Pine in about five hours. Since the only choices between the two routes were James' stomach lining or my eyes, and since I'm all about the well-being of others, this was an impossible choice. So, the only solution was to create a third alternative. Kind of like Captain Kirk and the Kobayashi Maru. But since my third choice added extensive time to the trip (three years in fact) and caused great pain (physically and mentally), but brought great comedy (many times at James' expense) and increased our self-awareness (we are now ready for the World's end), I don't believe anyone would say that we cheated.

Still, as I sat atop Mount Whitney at 11 o'clock with the sun warming my face that August morning, I wondered if the third alternative was the right path; was the direction we chose worth all the pain and all the gain. The view east certainly didn't support our decision. There's Lone Pine, some 10,000 feet below and beyond that is the Death Valley area, some 14,000 feet below. The view north and south certainly wasn't worth it. I mean all you see in those directions are the peaks of other mountains in the Sierra Nevada range; all below us. The view west is Kings Canyons National Park. A gorgeous park, when you're in it, but when you are thousands of feet above, its desolation. Bottom line, at 14,500 feet above sea level, the only things that grow are rocks and, unless you're a geologist, rocks are generally not beautiful and we were sitting atop a lot of not beautiful rocks. So, I wondered if the miles of backpacking, the blisters, the rain, the snow, the failures, the successes were worth this moment sitting atop Mount Whitney.

I quickly realized though, it wasn't the views that made this moment worth all our trials and tribulations; it wasn't even the achievement of reaching the summit. What made this moment special was the time James and I spent together over the three years it took us to reach the summit; the experiences we shared over those three years and the conversations that shaped our lives over those three years.

Now three years might sound like a long time, especially when you're talking about hiking to the top of a mountain, and three years might seem like an exaggeration, especially since we broke camp approximately nine hours earlier, but trust me, it took us three years and nine hours to summit Mount Whitney and the main reason for that was because we were/are average guys. We have wives, children, and regular guy jobs. I'm a mechanical engineer for a small manufacturing company in Fresno and James is a cubicle drone for a K-12 school district in Southern California. We didn't do anything special. Neither of us run, have a gym membership, or a designated "workout room" in our houses. We like to hang out, eat good (read: junk) food, watch good movies, and pontificate about what we would do in any situation if only given the chance. And like most average guys, we overestimate our abilities, our skill set, and completely underestimate the situation before us.

It also took us three years and nine hours to summit Whitney because when we started backpacking, Whitney was not on our minds….at all. We simply wanted to test ourselves, to be free from the trappings of society, to see if we could endure in the wilderness, on our own, for at least a weekend. And it took three years and nine hours to complete that test.

What you are about to read are the misadventures of two regular guys who thought, nay believed, they could do anything. Within these pages lie the road less traveled; well, because no one in their right minds would take that road. Unless, of course, you're talking about two schmucks.

TABLE OF CONTENTS

Top of the World 1
Alder Creek Trail Loop 7
    All Signs Point to Stop 7
    Two Schmucks 13
    Ranger Jane or Witch Jane 15
    A Bear with No Footprints 19
    The Fundamental Law of Backpacking 22
    A Payphone, a Civic, and Speed-Freak Tim 26
    When is an Adventure a Vacation 29
Victorious 31
    Lessons Learned and Ignored 31
    Yosemite Falls 34
    Laws Cannot Be Broken 39
    North Dome 40
    A New Rule 43
    Carol Comes to our Rescue 46
    Victory Comes at a Price 47
Winter Hits the Sierra Nevadas 49
    Let It Snow, Let It Snow, Let It Snow… 49
    We Head South 50
    Difference Makers 50
    "Left Turn Clyde" 53
    Mid 40's 55
Angeles Too Cold 58
    We Head West 58

- Omen of Things to Come 59
- Be Careful What You Wish For 62
- Shoes and Socks 64
- A Commitment Made 66

Girls Trip 68

Chilnualna Falls 74
- Alder Wins Again 74
- You'll Know It When You Hear It 77

A Moment in Time 80
- The Giant Forest 80
- Snow in the Lake 81
- An Assault 84

It's Still All About the Shoes 88
- Valley Floor 88
- Big Baldy 89
- Go On Without Me 92

Let's Ramp It Up 97
- Sleepy Hollow 97
- Difference Between Light and Dark 99

We Will Dominate 103
- The Best Lunch Spot in the Country 103
- Superman vs Lex Luthor 105

Hiking in Anticipation 111
- Cut This.... 111
- The Last Trip 115

Mount Whitney 119
- The Lottery 119

We Ascend 119
We Descend 125
To the Victor Goes the Prize 127

Alder Creek Trail Loop

All Signs Point to Stop

I couldn't believe what I just heard. Was she serious? "You know we're not going to come looking for you". Why would she say that? If they're not going to come looking, why are we filling out this registration card? Why would they have to come looking for us? Did the ranger call from the front gate and convince her to give us one final warning? These thoughts actually went through my head as we stood in the Wawona Ranger Station; but her warning, nor the ranger's warning at the front gate, would deter us, from backpacking the Alder Creek Loop that cloudy and ominous Saturday in September 2007. In hindsight, it may have been stupid to set off that morning, what with the warnings from the rangers and the storm clouds rolling in over the mountains, but I don't regret one minute of that weekend excursion.

About a month earlier, myself and James Johnson sat atop Garfield Peak in Crater Lake National Park near Klamath Falls, Oregon. We were deployed to Kingsley Field with our unit, the 144th Fighter Wing and, during the off weekend, decided to take a side trip to see just how blue this water was in the famed Crater Lake. For the record, it's pretty damn blue. While we there, looking over Wizard Island and the surreal blue water in the caldera; we stumbled upon a wonderful idea: wouldn't it be great to go backpacking? You know, just head off into the woods with only what you are willing, and can, carry on your back. Not an original idea I grant you, but something new for me and James. I don't know about James, but I love to challenge myself. I get a feeling of satisfaction from pushing myself to my limits and then finding the strength, either mental or physical, to go further. It's why I think it would be great to grind it out on one of those crab boats you see on Deadliest Catch or why I try to build a 40 x 15 deck in a weekend and it's why I wanted to go backpacking. Could I spend the weekend in the woods with only the items I brought? Could I overcome any hardships we might face? Hardships caused by nature; snow, rattlesnake bite, broken leg, or hardships caused by our own stupidity; not enough water, impractical shoes or heading into the woods when a ranger says, and I quote, "Are you crazy?" I don't know if going into this journey I was planning to push mine, and unfortunately James' limits, but because I like the idea of challenging myself, I'm sure that subconsciously I was going to do my best to turn each leisurely backpacking trip into a test of mental and physical endurance. On this particular sunny weekend, (note to others, don't be fooled by the sun in the morning) in September, that's exactly what I did.

Alder Creek was going to be our first backpacking trip. The Alder Creek Loop is located in Wawona, at the southwestern edge of Yosemite National Park, and is approximately 20 miles long and has about 4000 feet of elevation gain and loss across its entirety. This particular Loop is not strenuous for a seasoned backpacker or hiker, and a seasoned backpacker could probably do it in a day, certainly a weekend. Beginners on the other hand; well let's just say that we may have set our sights a little too high.

With our destination determined, we needed our gear. James was one up on me in this regard. He was all in from the moment we had the idea atop Garfield's Peak. So, he purchased his tent, backpack, camp stove, sleeping bag, and most importantly, shoes.

This brings us to rule number one of backpacking: *It's all in the Shoes.* Don't skimp on the shoes. Don't try and save a few dollars by going with something that "should" do. Splurge on the shoes. Spend more than you normally would. Make sure they fit, perfectly. Am I making my point here? Trust me when I tell you, *It's all in the Shoes.* A lesson I learned the hard way when at mile 6 of our adventure, my clodhoppers were filled with water and my feet were frozen. I may have digressed a little here but I want to make sure you understand how important it is to have the proper footwear.

As I said before, James already purchased his backpacking equipment. He bought books and researched what kind of gear to get, and what not to get. He read reviews and manufacturers specs and had everything shipped to his house so he could practice putting it all together. I, on the other hand, had nothing. See, I'm cheap. Some people politely say I'm frugal or careful with my money. But in the end, I'm cheap. Hence my understanding of the importance of proper footwear. My reluctance to part with my money also caused me not to want to purchase backpacking equipment until I determined that this was something, I wanted to do long term. So, I contacted a couple of sporting goods stores and checked into the cost to rent backpacking equipment. Even though renting gear is an inexpensive alternative to purchasing the gear, it is still more than a couple bucks, and therefore something that I didn't immediately embrace. I called James to see how much of his gear could also double as my gear. I mean, we are friends; known each other for a couple of years at that point. What the hell, share and share alike, right? After he feigned surprise at how careful I was with my money, he discussed the possibility of us sharing gear, and by discuss, I mean, he told me there was no way we would both fit in his tent and fit or not, we were not sharing his sleeping bag. Obviously, James wasn't going to help me, so back to renting. I rented a tent and sleeping bag. I purchased a backpack and cook stove. The shoes were a Christmas gift I got from my son two years before which I had never worn and although they were called Trailgear, they were not "trail rated", not good for hiking and should never have been used for backpacking; but I am cheap and I owned them, so they were on my feet when the river came rushing down the trail.

With gear in hand, we needed our food. James went with quick, easy to prepare meals; cans of Hormel Chili and Stew. Not the little plastic can that serves as a bowl that you pop in the microwave and heat for a quick snack. No, he went with the family size, two-pound steel can that when full can double as a hammer to pound in tent stakes. This clearly violated rule number 2 of backpacking, which if you don't already know is: *Lighter is Better.*

There is a huge difference in hauling a 35-pound pack for 8, 10 or 15 miles versus a 30-pound pack. Believe it. Every pound matters when you're hiking up a 20% grade at the beginning of the trip and down the same 20% grade at the end.

I, on the other hand, went to REI, the Cathedral of all that is backpacking. I swear that when I walk into REI, I hear organ music and a choir spiritiously singing the perfect "AHHHHHH". I almost weep. At REI I picked up a couple of freeze-dried meals: spaghetti and mac-n-cheese, lightweight and easy to prepare. Clearly too easy, makes too much sense and will certainly not live up to expectations.

Now with our destination chosen, which was more than we could handle, our gear purchased and/or rented, which for me was cheap and included shoes that were better suited for hiking the Magnificent Mile, and food stores secured, albeit impractical, we were ready to head out to conquer the Alder Creek Loop.

We left in good spirits at about six in the morning. It was still dark, but the previous night the weatherman called for sunny skies and temperatures in the mid-80's. That of course was the weather in Fresno. It was not the weather in Wawona. We did not know the weather in Wawona. Although I would not say it's a rule of backpacking, I will say that it's a good idea to know the weather of your destination. Just something to keep in mind. We arrived at the entrance to Yosemite at around 8 that morning and if we can argue that ignorance prevented us from seeing how fateful this trip was going to be; only pure stupidity spurred us on after we met the ranger at the gate.

She was a nice enough person. Probably in her late twenties or early thirties. Perhaps attractive but it's hard to tell in those dull green uniforms, Smokey-the-Bear hat and hair pulled back in a short ponytail. Ranger Jane, the name we give to all female rangers, greeted us and asked what brought us to Yosemite. I smiled my big toothy smile and with the exuberance of a 6-year-old sitting on Santa's lap I said, "We're going backpacking!!" With equal exuberance, albeit from a very different place, Ranger Jane replied, "Are you crazy?!!" Certainly not the response we expected. With a nervous laugh, I asked Jane, first name basis now, what she meant by that. Jane pointed out the storm clouds over the mountains, and explained that more were moving in. She also pointed out that we were wearing blue jeans and cotton shirts, not the kind of items to wear when backpacking, especially with storm clouds rolling in overhead.

Earlier, when discussing backpacking gear, I did not bring up clothes. Obviously, I never gave even a passing thought to my apparel. Purchasing "special" clothes for backpacking never entered my mind. I'm sure being cheap was part of the reason but also because I'm a man. A man that mows his own lawn, repairs his own car, builds monstrous decks, drinks way too many beers at night and simply does not shop for clothes…ever. James is also a man, but is a bit more practical. So, I believe he was better off than me in the clothes department, but as anyone can tell you that's been backpacking or even hiking when one suffers all suffer. Not so much a rule, but more of a truism.

Not to be deterred by Jane's voice of reason and experience, I explained to Ranger Jane that the storm clouds would be rolling in and out all day but probably never really threaten us and besides we were only taking the 20-mile loop. Therefore, at any given time, we wouldn't be too far from our vehicle. As for our clothes, what are a few extra pounds created by soaked jeans or shirts if it rains? We can handle the extra weight. Clearly, we had no clue about Rule 2. Off we went….

With Ranger Jane fading in the distance and her warnings sufficiently squashed, we proceeded to Wawona and the ranger station. In the ranger station we would fill out our registration card, so if we didn't return, they could come find us. Right? We were wrong on so many levels that day.

Here, we meet Ranger Jane #2. Remember we call all female rangers Ranger Jane. We got two pieces of information from the second Ranger Jane. First, she told us that, just yesterday, she hiked the full 20 miles of the Alder Creek Loop in one day. Since the second Ranger Jane looked at least 50, this bit of information bolstered our confidence and ensured that we would enter the hike with all the bravado needed to crash and burn. In hindsight, I now believe the second Ranger Jane was not 50 but probably in her mid-thirties and looked 50 because she hiked the Alder Creek Loop in one day. Second, Ranger Jane #2 told us that they would not come looking for us unless a family member told them we were missing. It turns out that the registration cards that must be filled out are only used to warrant that the trails do not go over their quotas for the day or weekend. No worries though, as our bravado would push us through this endeavor and see us safely to the other side. Before we left the ranger station and headed out on our fateful journey, the second Ranger Jane gave us one last thing to make certain that this trip would be a disaster: a bear canister.

To spend the night in the backcountry of Yosemite National Park, you must have: a bear canister. A bear canister is much like a pony keg and completely violates Rule number 2. Unfortunately, unlike a pony keg, a bear canister has no handles. It is completely smooth on all surfaces rendering it equivalent to something like a dog toy with goodies hidden inside. Subsequently, there is absolutely no way to effectively carry or stow a bear canister. The purpose of this medieval device is to stow your food, toothpaste, instant coffee, cocoa packets, empty chili cans, and/or anything that may or may not give off an odor that is attractive to the indigenous bruin population of the greater Yosemite region. Once all odorous items are placed in the canister, it is then chucked away from the campsite; at least 75 feet upon Ranger Jane's recommendation. If a bear happens upon the canister, their claws will not be able to grip the smooth exterior, thereby making it impenetrable, thus keeping the bear from adopting a diet of human food and toothpaste. I believe though that the canister is smooth so we will fight with it during the whole trip, refuse to bring food on future trips, thereby not spending the night and the park will have to worry less about overnight campers. Clearly, the second Ranger Jane and her cohorts are devious.

With all warnings, verbal and visual, sufficiently ignored and the 42-pound bear canister stowed atop James' backpack in a way that would certainly give him fits during the entire trip, we headed toward the trailhead of the Alder Creek Loop.

Two Schmucks

To provide a little context, The Alder Creek Loop progresses in the following manner: from the trailhead, it goes up. "Ascend" would be too gentle of a word. Rises doesn't do it justice either. The trail just goes up. At approximately the 8-mile mark, you reach Deer Creek Camp; a relatively flat area with a backcountry fire pit consisting of rocks arranged in a ring. A couple miles later there's a junction with Bridalveil Camp Trail. A mile beyond that is the high point of the trail. Three miles further is Chilnualna Falls where you go down, not "descend", but just go down to the town of Wawona. From there you can take the road back to the parking lot and your vehicle.

We hit the trailhead at approximately 9 in the morning. The sun was shining and it was warming up nicely. When we left the truck, it was probably in the 50's but soon enough it would be in the mid-70's. Clearly, all the warnings were nothing more than lesser folk attempting to undermine our ambitions. We had the sun in our face, the soft ground at our feet and the confidence necessary to guarantee that we would continue to ignore all signs of imminent peril. We were men of strength and destiny; men on their own in the wilderness, taking on nature; sure, of not only surviving but dominating. We were…… Two Schmucks.

Cameron Williams, aka Schmuck 1

Three hours up, our breathing was labored, my feet were aching, my ankles were throbbing, and we were so hunched over that we needed a chiropractor to straighten us out. And, what did we have to show for it? Three Miles. But we knew our first trip would be hard. Besides, the sun was shining and it was lunchtime. We knew things would get better after a much-needed break for something to eat. James had a sandwich and Cheddar Goldfish for lunch. He always has good lunches. He's smarter than I am when it comes to food; except of course for his cans of stew and chili. James brings flatbread, something that doesn't get crushed in his backpack, and some sort of a spread. He also brings Goldfish or Cheez-It crackers. I love those things so it's great that he's always willing to share. I think I ate trail mix, or an orange, or some pudding. My lunches are always lame and unsatisfying. I need to work on my lunches. It was a good break though. The sun was shining and,

James Johnson, aka Schmuck 2

even though we were behind, we were in good spirits and still believed that we could make The Loop in two days. Our confidence, our sheer bravado was strong that day.

After lunch, we continued to head up, not "ascend", head up Alder Creek Loop. A very large bear crossed the trail not 10 yards in front of us. It didn't stop nor gave us a second glance. It was just passing by. It was a cool moment. It was the first time I saw a bear in the wild. Somewhere around noon, we reached a small ribbon of a waterfall. I believe it was Alder Creek dumping over a cliff. It started drizzling around this point. Nothing more than a mist. We stopped and put on our Gore-Tex® jackets. After all, we weren't completely clueless and used the time to snap a few photos.

Ranger Jane or Witch Jane

From small "Alder Creek Falls" to Deer Creek Camp I have no remembrance of time nor space. I don't know when it began to rain, or when the rain turned to snow, or when the snow turned to ice, or when the ice turned back to rain, or when the cycle began again. I don't know how long either type of precipitation lasted, but I know it never ended. I don't know where on the trail we were as these meteorological events unfolded because all I saw of the trial was the immediate 12 inches in front of my lousy, cheap, soaked, shoes.

When it first began to rain, I thought how refreshing it was. Living in Fresno, I don't see much rain so it's nice to feel its cooling wetness on your face. Not like a child on a hot summer day raising his face to the coolness of an afternoon drizzle. More like an adult who was sweating like he had been hiking up-hill all damn day with a 30 pound back on his back. Also, the Gore-Tex® went on when it was drizzling and Gore-Tex® doesn't breathe, so a little stiff rain and a slight drop in temperature were appreciated. The problem with the rain though, is everything gets wet and that includes the three-foot tall ferns that line The Alder Creek Loop Trail. As we walked along in the rain, our torsos sufficiently protected, my legs would drag through those wet ferns and my jeans were getting soaked. No longer was the rain refreshing; it had become another force trying to deter us from completing the now more and more formidable Alder Creek Loop. The rain had turned the trail to mud and had begun to find its way through any small opening of our Gore-Tex® and backpacks. Before too long I was cursing the rain. Fortunately, we didn't have to put up with the rain forever.

By the time the rain turned to snow, my jeans weighed as much as the bear canister sitting upon James' backpack. Unfortunately, the snow was no reprieve from the wetness of the rain. In fact, the snow added another element to our trip. Not only was the trail now mud but the snow made the trail slick. Maybe not for James in his trail rated hikers, but certainly for me in my downtown, Trailgear, Christmas presents. My feet would have been just as protected in the box that housed the shoes. Onward we pressed. The bravado was still strong. We marched up the trail, and I sometimes slid back and marched on again. Besides making the trail slick, another fine attribute of the snow was its ability to accumulate. It amassed on my head, my hands, and my backpack. Rule number 2 was taking a beating. So, like the rain before it, it wasn't too long before I was cursing the snow. Fortunately, like the rain, we didn't have to put up with the snow forever.

Remember earlier when I said I only saw the 12 inches of the trail directly in front of my shoes? That wasn't because I was so beaten, I couldn't pick my head up. I kept my head down because I was afraid that one of the shards of ice raining from the sky would take out my eye! Small, hard, jagged, not-of-this-earth, chunks of ice falling from the sky. Well, falling might not be the right word. *Jettisoned* from the sky is more descriptive of what we were feeling with the shards raining down on us from above. It was Ranger Jane and all of her witchcraft practicing friends. Because, by now, it was clearly Ranger Jane's fault that we were in this predicament. We just knew that they had summoned some meteorological demon to force us to turn back just to prove that she, Ranger Jane, was correct. But we were not going to be forced back by rain, snow, or ice. The Postal Service has nothing on these Two

Schmucks. Slick, muddy, uphill trails were not going to stop us. A bear canister the size of a Volkswagen Beetle and jeans made of lead were not going to make us abandon our quest. We were…. Two Schmucks.

Luckily, like the snow before and the rain before that, the ice didn't last forever and by now, you should know where this is headed. Now that the trail was muddy and covered in snow it wouldn't take much to turn our uphill trail into a raging, downhill river; a fact that proved itself as soon as the ice turned back to rain. Clearly, I'm exaggerating when I call our trail a raging river. At best it was a gushing stream, which is still not good when you're wearing hiking shoes made for Christmas shopping at the Glendale Galleria. Even James' practical, trail rated hiking boots were no match for the water running down the hill to meet our every step. Of course, we could have avoided the stream by walking off the trail; which we tried from time to time, as the terrain allowed, but with the snow and ice and the roughness of the terrain, the stream was actually the safest path. As the water ran over our boots and covered our feet with what was literally ice water, I remember thinking two things; first – my feet are frozen and I'm going to have to chop them off and second – there need to be rules for backpacking; hence, rule number one followed closely by rule number two.

As we slogged along, the rain began to change to snow, which would be followed by ice and then rain again, the sun began to set and I began to realize that it is going to get dark and we are going to die on this trail. Obviously, we didn't die because this is non-fiction, but the thought crossed my mind.

It was getting dark fast and we were not even at the mid-way point, not at the high point of the trail, and not carried on the wings of confidence and bravado. We needed to start thinking of bedding down for the night and hoping that the storm would allow us to pack out in the morning.

At about this time in our self-realization, we came around the bend and there was Deer Creek Camp. As mentioned earlier, Deer Creek Camp is a relatively flat backcountry clearing featuring a fire pit. Deer Creek

Camp also had a grove of about 5 trees. Had is precisely right; more on that to follow. The fire pit was, of course, useless as all available wood was soaked to the core, covered in snow, and frozen together. However, the small grove of trees could provide some shelter from the meteorological Armageddon descending upon us. There in the small grove, a calm came over me.

A few times during the hike James asked me what we should do, continue on or turn around. This question would come up whenever we got tired of trudging through the rain or snow or ice. Each time the question came up though, I would just point forward and off we would go. I didn't choose forward because I thought it was best, or because I didn't want to fail. I chose forward because I simply didn't know what else to do. But in the grove of trees, it was different. When James asked then, I took a breath, really thought about the situation and realized that we could die if we kept trying to move forward and therefore the best thing to do would be to make camp. Truth be told, we probably could have hiked on through the night in those conditions; after all, we aren't elderly or in poor health, but the point is, I was able to gain my composure, push aside the distractions, and think clearly about our situation. What a wonderful feeling that was; I think it was my first real feeling of leadership. Whenever things around me are in chaos, I think back to that moment and it allows me to compose myself, make a decision, and move forward.

I've read a few books on leadership over the years and I don't recall one that states in order to be a good leader you need to lead. That's odd to me because how can anyone be a good leader unless they lead? I don't care if you subscribe to the theory that great leaders are born or if you think moments make great leaders; in either case, the only way to improve is to do and James has always allowed me to lead. That night, in the grove of trees at Deer Creek Camp, I think I might have finally met his expectations. On the other hand, I did lead him eight miles into the woods through rain, snow, and ice and it was 50/50 as to whether we were going to make it out alive, so perhaps I'm a little too arrogant.

In either case, it was there that we made camp; eight miles from the trailhead; approximately 7 ½ hours in; for the math curious, that equates to about 1 mile per hour. As I lay in my tent that evening, I remember thinking threes things; Rule number 1, Rule number 2 and we suck at backpacking.

A Bear with No Footprints

That night at camp was uneventful if you disregard the smoke-filled tents and the footless bear.

We decided to set-up our tents in the grove of what were 5 trees, completely ignoring the fact that the trees were being covered in ice and snow. Obviously, the goal was to erect the tents without any water getting in the tents, kind of a useless plan since everything we owned, including the tents, were soaked. Surprisingly though, I was able to erect my tent with very little water getting into the tent. James' tent, on the other hand, needed a Wet-Dry Vac. I first realized his tent was underwater when I heard the distinctive sound of a wash rag being wrung dry. Think of cleaning up a spill on the floor or counter with a rag. You run the rag over the spill and then ring out the rag. That is exactly what James was doing on the floor of his tent with a bandanna. Wipe and ring out; wipe and ring out; repeat; over and over. I'm sure it took him over thirty minutes to dry the floor of his tent. I guess he did not practice putting up his tent in a torrential downpour. In the end, though, both of us were out of the elements safely enclosed by 1mm of nylon. Nothing could hurt us now.

I didn't pay much attention to the smoke rising from my little cook stove. Actually, the fire itself is smokeless as I was using a can of Sterno. Also, I had the cook stove near the front of the tent, which was opened slightly. The smoke was being generated by items in the tent drying and by the contents of my freeze-dried food. However, when the wind shifted and blew into the tent, then I paid a lot of attention to the smoke. I really had no choice since it was blinding me. Granted, most of it was water vapor but when you can't see and have a fire in a nylon tent, you tend to freak-out. I kept my composure though, found the zipper to the tent opening, and opened it further. I know at first this might not seem smart after all the wind was blowing into the tent. But I knew that the wind would shift, and when it would, it would take the smoke from my tent. Five minutes later, the wind of course shifted and my tent was cleared.

Now to be completely honest, I didn't fully keep my composure while encapsulated by smoke. I was shouting out to James for assistance, who it turns out was dealing with his own coffin of death. Remember James brought a can of chili and a can of stew for dinner. Once on the burner of his cook stove, not only did his tent fill with the water vapors of everything drying but also with the smoke pouring out of his dinner. Luckily though, like my tent, his tent was evacuated of smoke when the wind shifted.

By that time our dinners were ready to eat, or at least James' was ready. Mine, on the other hand, was partially overcooked and partially raw. Not the best situation when eating mac-n-cheese. Freeze dried food requires water; which we had plenty. However, it was dark outside when I was preparing my meal so I could not tell how much water to add. Also, because of my bout with the smoke, I could not tell when the water I did add began to boil. So, after the smoke cleared, I decided it was time to eat, which of course it was not, and spent the next few minutes alternating between mac-n-cheese soup and raw pasta. Just so you know, I have tried freeze dried meals on other trips and none of them were successful. I have since abandoned freeze dried meals.

With our bellies full and our gear starting to dry out, it was time to turn in. I have no idea what time it was when I crawled into my sleeping bag, but I didn't care because I was exhausted and I knew I would sleep like a baby. How many times in one weekend could I be wrong?

Before we could truly turn in for the night though, we needed to place everything that had a scent into our bear canister. So, we gathered up our trail mix and toothpaste and coffee and anything else that smelled, forced it all into the bear canister and chucked the canister as far as we could from our tent site; about 4 feet. The canister landed with a resounding thud right in front of our tents. I swear I felt my tent shake when it landed. After our laughing fit subsided, James stepped out into the snow and cold air and ran the canister about 100 feet and then threw it. Now the canister was 104 feet from the tent. Far enough.

Now, I have no idea how long it took before the bear came crashing into our campsite. I'm not even sure if it was the sound of the bear's paws crunching through the frozen earth that woke me. Even though I was completely exhausted, I could not sleep for more than twenty minutes before one of my limbs would "go to sleep" caused by the frozen earth cutting off circulation to that extremity. What I do know is that the noise was very loud and very distinctive. There was a bear in our campsite and he was looking for food. Luckily our food was in an impenetrable bear canister a good 104 feet away. I called out to James in the loudest whisper I dared with a 4,000-pound bear at my door, "James"!

He replied, "What?" Also, in a whisper. Clearly, James had heard the prowler.

"Do you hear that?"

"Yes"

"Is it a bear?"

"I think so."

"Go check it out."

"No."

There was no more conversation. We continued to listen to the bear as it stomped around Deer Creek Camp until we heard a loud crash. The crash obviously signifying that the bear found our bear canister, became completely agitated that he could not open the treasure trove of toothpaste, trail mix, and the crushed remnants of canned chili and ran off into the woods breaking frozen branches and frozen three-foot tall ferns.

"James, do you think he's gone?" I whispered.

"I think so", James replied.

"Go check it out."

"No."

Conversation over, and so was the sleep. The rest of the night, between the frozen ground, my damp sleeping bag, and the immediate threat from a marauding black bear, I slept very little.

We climbed out of our tents the next morning to find partially sunny skies, horrific leg cramps, still soaked clothing and no bear tracks. How could there be no bear tracks? We walked all over Deer Creek Camp and found no bear tracks. Our bear canister was still where James tossed it. Then we saw our bear. Remember the grove of 5 trees? Now the grove was 4. The fifth tree was still there but the weight of the ice in the branches caused the tree to snap at its base and fall directly over James' tent. What we heard was the trunk slowly giving way and the loud crash was the tree falling through the surrounding trees. Fortunately, a couple sturdy branches caught the tree approximately four feet from the top of James' tent. If not for those branches, James would have backpacked only one time in his life and I would have had to deliver the worst news of my life. We had a lot of bad luck on this trip, but when it counted most, someone was looking out for us!

The Fundamental Law of Backpacking

After giving thanks for what could be classified as a miracle, we decided to build a fire. Of course, this may have seemed hopeless, but the sun was shining a little and we thought maybe our luck had turned, and we were able to start a fire. Not a strong fire, but enough to stand around and drink coffee and hot chocolate. Besides, we needed a fire to dry our clothes.

With all our gear packed, James and I stood on the rocks that ringed our fire pit, face to face. We threw our hands over each other's shoulders to stabilize ourselves. We stood like that, looking like two equally matched wrestlers; neither one able to move the other. The fire burned between us and our clothes began to dry. The smoke rising between us, caused by our drying clothes, was so thick we could not see each other's face even though we were inches apart. If someone happened down the trail at that time, they would have thought there were two witches burning at the stake. I couldn't help thinking about Ranger Janes 1 and 2. We did not stay that way until we were completely dry, but certainly long enough to notice a difference in the weight of our clothes and gear. By that time, it was about 9 in the morning and it was time to complete The Loop

In good spirits, pounds lighter, and a little bit of sun shining upon us we started up the trail. Unfortunately, our good spirits and the trail did not last long. Yesterday's events may not have washed the trail completely away, but between the running water and snow, most of the trail was gone and what was left was barely discernible. I took off ahead of James who had lingered behind to relieve himself of the morning coffee. The time it took the coffee to leave his system was time enough for us to get separated. I had strayed off the trial and when James began to call my name, I knew he was also wandering around in the ferns and manzanita. For those not familiar with manzanita, it is a generally short, dense bush that has beautiful bronze, smooth bark, and small green leaves. Manzanita also has thorns like the claws of velociraptors, the small, human hunting dinosaurs from Jurassic Park. Unfortunately, we were separated by a grove of these pants shredding, skin tearing bushes. I give it James though, unable to locate the trail, and knowing I was standing directly above him on the trail, he proceeded to force his way through the brush following the sound of my voice. When he emerged on my side of the manzanita grove, surprisingly unscathed from the vicious thorns, he had once again gained all water weight lost early that day while around the fire. James was now 15 pounds heavier than he was 20 minutes earlier and still had the Volkswagen strapped to the top of his backpack. A good friend would have offered to take the weight of the bear canister; I, of course, did not for I completely understood rule number 2. No matter though, we had a hike to complete and the sun was still peeking through the clouds so once again, we continued up the trail.

I need to provide Rule number 3 before I go any further. Rule number 3, in deference to Sir Isaac Newton, is called the Fundamental Law of Backpacking, or in slang, *What Goes Down Must Go Up*. As the story goes, Sir Isaac postulated the Fundamental Law of Gravity when an apple fell from a tree and hit him on the head. I'm sure though that Sir Isaac suffered no pain in his discovery as he probably actually only witnessed an apple falling. We, on the other hand, experienced copious amounts of pain discovering our law.

Backpacking in the Sierra Nevada is all about elevation gain and loss. Since in most cases, you end your hike where you started your hike, you will gain or lose elevation in the beginning and then lose or gain the same elevation in the end. Also, there is always a high point on the trail. The high point is not always in the middle of the hike. In fact, mileage wise, it is rarely in the middle of the hike. However, since it is the high point, it's always downhill from the high point until the end. Knowing this, you drive towards the high point. You gage your ability to reach the end by measuring what's left in your tank when you reach the high point. So needless to say, when the trail goes down before reaching the high point, it is a little disconcerting since now you have to make up the elevation that was just lost. The elevation that was gained at the price of stamina and muscle. Elevation you don't want to return because no one is going to give you back the strength you used to gain that elevation. And on this hike, to say giving up elevation was a little disconcerting is like saying King Kong was a little ape.

The schmuck's look says it all

We are clear on the Fundamental Rule of Backpacking? Very well then, we started up the trail. I understand that sometimes "up" may mean north or away from the starting point or just simply forward, but in this case, it meant up; and more up than at any other time of our hike. If we were on this part of the trail yesterday, when the water was running down towards us, that water would have been a waterfall. The reason why the trail was so steep here is that as we entered the camp last night, we were walking downhill. Now we needed to gain back the lost elevation plus we still haven't reached the high point of the trail, and we never would.

This part of the trail broke me and I know it broke James. As we trudged up the hill, stopping every six feet to catch our breath and relieve the pain in our legs it was becoming clear that we were not going to complete The Formidable and now Unforgiving Alder Creek Loop Trail. This meant turning back and walking the eight miles from which we came. Certainly doable, since in general the hike would be downhill, but I had a better idea, an idea that would get us back to our car more expeditiously, an idea, like all previous ideas, that would certainly lead to great pain for both of us.

According to my map, Bridalveil Camp Trail intersected our trail about halfway up the hill and in a few steps, thirty minutes in time, we reached that junction. I postulated that by taking Bridalveil Camp Trail we would get to the Bridalveil Campground in less than an hour and some caring camper would give us a ride back to our vehicle. A perfect plan; except for the fact that when we got to the campground it was closed for the winter and completely devoid of campers, caring or otherwise.

A Payphone, a Civic, and Speed-Freak Tim

Our spirits which were good that morning, what with the sunshine and lighter clothes, and bolstered by my flawless plan, were now lower than the seventh level of Dante's hell. We were so low at this point, that all we could do was laugh. We were laughing at our misfortune and imminent demise, for now, we had to go back not eight miles, or nine miles, but 11 miles of punishing trail; back the way we came. Clearly, we were going insane and chances were good that one of us would turn to cannibalism before this adventure was over.

But as is so often the case, when things are at their lowest, something occurs that restores hope and makes you believe that you can succeed and for us, that something was a pay phone. There was a pay phone on the road at the entrance to the campground. Surprisingly we had change in our pocket, but of course no phone number to the ranger station. Information was happy to provide that number though and after a slight pause, we were connected to Ranger Jane 3. She could have been the original Ranger Jane or even Ranger Jane 2, but chances are, since she never said, "I told you so", she was a new Ranger Jane and hence Ranger Jane number 3.

We told Ranger Jane 3 our plight, in full detail, and asked her to send a vehicle post-haste to give us a ride to freedom, to which she asked, "Is it an emergency?" I really thought we drove that point home, what with talk of broken spirits and cramping legs and rushing water and frozen feet and shattered backs, but when faced with the question directly, I could not honestly say that it was. We told Ranger Jane number 3 that there were no broken bones and no one was dying, but we did express our concern that one of us might die if we didn't get out of there soon.

Ranger Jane then told us to do something I haven't done since the '80's, "Walk to Glacier Point Road and hitchhike." What a great idea. Made even greater because I didn't think of it, for let's face it, my ideas sucked. We would walk to Glacier Point Road, about two miles on a relatively flat roadway, stick out our thumbs, get a ride to our car and be at the Oakhurst McDonald's in no time. Once again.... Wrong.

Hiking out to Glacier Point Road was uneventful, except for the rain now descending upon us. Unfortunately, hitchhiking on Glacier Point Road was also uneventful. Not that cars weren't available. There were no fewer than 50 cars, trucks, and vans driving by us that day. Not slowing down. Certainly not stopping, just driving by us; two backpackers, soaking wet, one carrying a Volkswagen on his back. We were......Two Schmucks.

What made this situation worse, as if it could be, was not the rain falling hard and steady, or the fact that the roadway was not a roadway at all but a rollercoaster, or the fact that we were now a full 30 miles from our car.; it was the combination of all three! In the woods, we were 11 miles max from our car; straight through the forest, downhill all the way. Now we were on Glacier Point Road, which intersected with Wawona Road and went around the forest. The 30 miles might have been doable if not for the fifteen-foot drops followed by 17-foot rises followed by 10-foot drops and 8 foot rises and so on and so on; not to mention the whole time we were trudging up and down the road we were getting heavier and heavier due to the rain soaking into our not-made-for-hiking clothes. At this point, this one moment in time, we were violating the first three rules of backpacking and we both knew we were going to spend another night in Yosemite National Park; another night in a smoke-filled tent, pitched on the frozen tundra, below ice covered trees. If we were lucky though, during the night, the forest would fall on our tents and put an end to our misery.

But, like the pay phone earlier, hope would appear out of nowhere. This time, that hope was in the shape of a white, Honda Civic. Frank, I frankly don't remember if that was actually the driver's name, but it's a good name, was retired Army and he and his wife were driving through Yosemite visiting the park from the comfort of their car, taking photos through rolled down windows. I always cuss those people and make fun of them, but today, of course, I had nothing but love for the drive-thru tourist named Frank.

Frank's car was small, only slightly larger than the bear canister James had so dutifully hauled through the woods. I can imagine the look on Frank's wife's face when he saw two drowned men carrying backpacks hitchhiking and said to his wife, "Honey I'm going to stop and give them a ride. I'm sure they can fit in the back seat". I'm sure the look on her face was identical to the look on the original Ranger Jane when some 29 hours earlier we told her we were going backpacking. Luckily for us, Frank ignored the look from his wife, pulled over and James and I gladly clambered into the backseat. We had to sit with our backs to each other facing the doors, with our backpacks on our laps, but we fit in Frank's white, sent from heaven Honda Civic.

The five-mile ride down Glacier Point Road was dry, smooth and full of laughter as we relayed the previous day's events to Frank and his wife. I cannot say the same for the 25-mile ride down Wawona Road.

Speed-freak Tim sold soda products and one of his regulars was the General Store in Yosemite Village. After stocking that store, and apparently slamming a couple Red-Bulls and Monster drinks, he was on his way out of Yosemite National Park when he stopped to use the restroom at the intersection of Wawona and Glacier Point Roads. Perfect timing for us, as Army Frank was heading into the valley and could only take us to said intersection. So as Frank dropped us off, Tim was exiting the restroom; what perfect luck. Once again though, there was a price to pay.

When we ran into Speed-Freak Tim coming out of the bathroom and asked him for a ride, how could he refuse? After all, he was on what was now a deserted road, with his back to a restroom and facing two men that would have certainly killed him rather than spend another night in

Yosemite, and I'm sure he saw that in our eyes. So, off the three of us went in Speed-Freak Tim's red, Ford Taurus, I in the passenger seat and James in the backseat behind Tim.

A 25-mile trip in Yosemite takes about an hour as the turns are tight and there are many dips and dives. Speed-Freak Tim covered the 25 miles in fifteen minutes. I don't know if it was fear of his two haggard and desperate passengers or Red-bull and Monster or the fact Speed-Freak Tim was clearly a meth-head; but fifteen minutes later, James and I were in the parking lot where we had parked the previous day. We were moving so fast, that I could not stop laughing as James was literally thrown from side to side in the back seat of the Death Race Taurus. A few years back, me, my wife and some friends were driving back from Lake Tahoe and we decided to take the mountain roads versus the highway. At some point, and I don't remember why I'm sure my wife does, I thought it would be cool to go around the turns fast enough to make the angel hanging from the rear-view mirror swing into a horizontal position. I never could attain that speed in my PT Cruiser with my wife and passengers screaming at me, but Speed-Freak Tim had no problem reaching that speed or centrifugal vectors, and James was paying the price. I, on the other hand, had an oh-shit handle to hold onto or I would have found myself in Speed-Freaks Tim's lap.

When is an Adventure a Vacation

We threw our gear in the back of the truck and our Gore-Tex® jackets in the back seat. The rain had stopped and the sun was coming out and the temperature was rising quickly; of course. We climbed in and started talking and laughing about the adventure. My legs were so sore; I could not push in the clutch. James' muscles were so sore, he could not roll down the window, something I thought was hysterical until I realized that I could not muster the strength to roll down my window. Eventually, though, we were able to roll down our windows and I was able to push in the clutch and we drove out of Yosemite National Park.

Our attempt to hike The Formidable and Unforgiving Alder Creek Trail Loop was certainly miserable and a complete failure. It was also a great weekend and possibly the best thing that could have happened to us. James and I are friends, both from the Chicago area, both members of the Air National Guard, and both out-of-place in California. But that weekend made us good friends if not great friends. We were still in the truck driving back to Fresno when we decided to hit the trail again in October and we continued hitting the trails every month. In fact, we returned to The Alder Creek Trail a few years later and completed the entire twenty-mile loop, with backpacks, in one day. But, that's another story.

It's easy when things go as planned; but when things go sideways, when you have to reach down for a little more, that's when you find your strength, your courage, your sense-of-humor and your will to continue. Our trip on Alder Creek Trail was our time on the crab boats of Alaska, it was our adventure. Like Vito the Guru says, "Without hardships, it's not an adventure, it's a vacation", and Alder Creek Loop was a great adventure.

Victorious

Lessons Learned and Ignored

Roughly a month following our Alder Creek Trail Loop Spectacular, we were ready for our next adventure and chomping at the bit to get back into the woods. That may sound crazy after our complete failure at Alder Creek Trail, but we wanted to try again; we needed to try again; we needed to pit ourselves against Mother Nature, against our own stupidity, and this time, do more than just survive. This time we needed to reach our goal, to declare ourselves victorious.

While our previous adventure may have been a complete failure, it was not a complete loss. We learned that when we thought we reached our limit, there was more in us; more confidence, more strength and yes, unfortunately, more stupidity. That's why we took up backpacking, not because we were full of stupidity, but because we wanted to test ourselves, to find our limits and then see if we could push further. Our first debacle in the woods taught us that we could overcome and we could endure. This trip, our second trip, and on some levels our second debacle as this trip would also have great moments of stupidity, would teach us that we could succeed.

On a personal note, during our last adventure, I learned that I wanted to pursue backpacking on a regular basis. So, there would be no rental equipment in my backpack during our hike up North Dome. I purchased myself a two-person backpacking tent, just-in-case my wife would ever want to join us and because a normal size human, someone over five feet tall and 65 pounds, would never fit into a one-person backpacking tent. A one-person backpacking tent is an oxymoron unless you consider a hobbit a person. I also purchased my own sleeping bag. I didn't put much thought into the sleeping bag. Most of them are rated for 20 degrees to 0 degrees. Since I wasn't planning on sleeping on Mount McKinley or in a snow igloo, I was confident a 20-degree bag would suffice. As the Alder Creek Spectacular clearly illustrated, I have no issues with confidence. Correctness, on the other hand, is something I'm struggling with, a fact that would prove itself during one exceptionally cold evening in the Angeles National Forest. But I digress. On to North Dome.

The Battle at Alder Creek gave way to what is now known as Vito's Maxim; which states: the feeling of joy that comes with the completion of an adventure is directly proportional with the adversities that must be overcome during said adventure. Obviously, for our second backpacking adventure, we needed a trail that would test our new-found limits, a trail, a trail that was 17 miles out and back and 2 miles up and down, a trail rated strenuous for day-hikers and therefore "not recommended" for backpacking; a trail sure to provide maximum misery Enter the North Dome via Yosemite Falls Trail. I'd like to think it was Vito's Maxim that caused us to choose this self-imposed death march; but it is far more likely that once again, we were overconfident and just plain stupid.

It's not surprising that our swagger was in full effect after the failure at Alder Creek. After all, it wasn't our fault. After that hike, we analyzed the situation thoroughly, if not honestly, and none of our theories including our lack of experience, lack of strength or lack of good thought held any water. Our theories ranged from Ranger Jane and her witch's coven to something including immaturity, drinking and broken promises to a higher being. Clearly, none of these theories included anything we could control, and since Ranger Jane and her cohorts proved their point and all past discrepancies were paid for, we had no reason not to head back into the woods and more importantly, absolutely no reason to ensure that we pick a destination aligned with our abilities. Besides, if we picked a destination suited for two schmucks like us, we would have hiked across the parking lot to Best Buy.

So, with the weather checked the night before, another lesson learned, our blue jeans abandoned for nylon convertibles, Alder Creek lesson number five, and backpacks thrown in the back of the truck, James and I headed to Yosemite Valley shortly after seven a.m. on a cool, crisp Saturday in October. Although we had implemented a number of lessons learned while getting our asses handed to us at Alder Creek, we were not smart enough to implement all of the lessons learned. Most notably, cans of stew and chili are not conducive to successful backpacking, freeze-dried food will always end in a mixture of sloppiness and crunchiness and footwear is the most important factor when it comes to backpacking. As hard as it may be to believe, James still had his cans of Hormel, I once again purchased freeze dried food from REI, and worst of all, I was still wearing shoes made by The Devil's Cobblers.

With a couple lessons implemented and Rules Number One and Two sufficiently ignored, we arrived at the front gate to Yosemite and was greeted by Ranger Rick (of course, it should go without saying, that we call all male rangers, Ranger Rick). Seeing Ranger Rick was a good sign. He did not ask us if we were crazy, he did not point out our impending doom caused by storms, and he clearly was not a witch. Things were looking up for us; until we arrived at the Ranger Station.

Two bad things happened at the Ranger Station; Ranger Jane (one, two, three, or new, who cares, they're all witches) greeted us and we received our state of the art, completely unwieldy, heavier than a micro-minibus, bear canister. As I look back, I am amazed that after our first encounter with the completely useless bear canister, we would subject ourselves; or more correctly, James would subject himself, to the unique torture that is known as "the hauling of the canister". I can assure you that this trip would be the last trip that either of us were ever again tortured by that black, smooth, useless, pony keg. But on this trip, James had the canister securely fastened to the top of his backpack as we headed to the North Dome trailhead.

North Dome, for the geologically curious, is the lesser known, and therefore the lesser hiked, of the two domes that rise above Yosemite Valley. Half Dome, North Dome's famous cousin, gets all the play. So much in fact, that hiking Half Dome is now limited to 400 people per day. Although Half Dome is very popular, there is one drawback, besides all the people you meet on the trail; you cannot see Half Dome from the top of Half Dome. North Dome, on the other hand, sits directly across the valley from the Yosemite icon and provides for a spectacular view. Also, very few people hike to the top of North Dome, especially if you start from the base of Yosemite Falls. There are two ways to the top of North Dome; drive up Tioga Road and hike down a 4.5-mile trail or, drive down to Yosemite Valley, hike 3.5 miles up Yosemite Falls and then hike five miles up to North Dome. Of course, we chose the hike that was "not recommended" for backpacking and would surely break us. So, at about 9:30 we found ourselves standing at the base of Yosemite Falls with footwear laced by the devil himself, backpacks loaded with regrettable dinners, and a bear canister that may or may not make it back from this trip.

Yosemite Falls

Hundreds of people visit Yosemite Falls every day. It is a wondrous sight as the Yosemite River tumbles over the cliff and falls three-quarters of a mile to the valley floor, stopping only once in a large basin approximately two-thirds of the way down. The vast majority of daily visitors hike up Yosemite Falls, or more correctly, attempt to hike up Yosemite Falls. You see, the trail from the valley floor to the top of the falls covers approximately 3.5 miles with a 3600-foot elevation gain. For all you masochists out there, that is almost a 20% grade. To reduce the steepness of the climb, the trail starts out with 1,200 switchbacks. Of course, that's an exaggeration, the actual number is probably closer to 100, but once you're in them, who cares how many there are. All you know is that you are doing a lot of walking with very little to show for it. I think it's better to just have the trail go straight up instead of winding back and forth. Of course, when the trail is going straight up, I wish it was winding back and forth. I don't see this as an indication that I'm hard to please but more an indication that whatever hell am in at the moment, I wish I was in a different hell.

Most hikers who begin the trek get through the switchbacks and arrive at the basin which is the top of the lower falls. When the water is at full flow in early spring, you will get soaked while standing around this basin. The refreshing water will bolster your confidence enough to continue on up the trail. However, very quickly, the trail will show you who's the boss. Beyond the lower falls, the trial is not so much a trail, as a trough created by two mountains coming together. The hike is basically straight up and stretches over and around rocks that have tumbled down the mountainside and became lodged in the trough. Steps have been added in places to reduce the vertical ascent, but in some ways, the steps have made the hike harder as the spacing between the steps will cause you to change your gait, which wreaks havoc on your knees. Most of the hikers that start up Yosemite Falls never see this part of the trail, and most that see this part, don't see the end. There are some though, that push through the countless switchbacks, up, over and around the rocks, and up the stairs to the top of Yosemite Falls. We were planning on being one of those few, the difference was, we were going to do it with 35 pounds on our back.

Now, to be honest, we knew nothing about the multitude of switchbacks, or the rocks, or the stairs. What we did know was that to get to the top of North Dome, we first needed to get to the top of Yosemite Falls. So off we went, up the trail, with my shoes from the Underworld and our bear canister from Mordor. Three switchbacks in we knew another disaster might be in our future.

Switchbacks seem like a good idea. They're cut into a hillside, or mountainside, in such a way that you zig-zag back and forth, slowly gaining elevation each time, thus cutting down on the vertical gain per step. However, I think switchbacks were created as a cruel joke. When you look at them, it seems easy, they appear level; you're confident you can make this hike without a problem. Therein lies the joke. You cannot make the hike without a problem. The switchbacks are not level, they are inclined so that you continue to gain elevation and then where the zig and zag meet you actually take a step up and gain the most elevation. So you end up forcing yourself up one zig to the next zag and at the junction point, take a step up. Then force yourself up the zag to the next zig and take a step up. Imagine repeating this process for 1200 zigs and zags with 35 pounds on your back and you have the first mile. You read that right, the first mile of our hike. We started up Yosemite Falls at 9:30 and by 10:30 we had finally reached the basin of Lower Yosemite Falls.

Once again, we were backpacking up the falls in October, so the falls were little more than a mist falling from above. Therefore, we were not refreshed by spraying water but our confidence was bolstered nonetheless. You see the trail around the Lower Yosemite Falls basin is generally level. Our muscles were given a much-needed reprieve as we traveled along the top of the lower falls. Alas, this reprieve was short lived as we began to ascend again.

As mentioned previously, as you begin the hike from the lower falls to the upper falls, the trail is really no more than a trough between two mountains. Now, there are some steps cut into what some may call switchbacks. I wouldn't call them switchbacks. I mean, if we call the switchbacks at the beginning of trail switchbacks than the so-called switchbacks at the middle of the trail cannot be called switchbacks. If you have to stop every ten steps and take a fifteen-second break, then you're not hiking on a switchback. If the switchback has steps cut into it because without them the steepness would be impossible to ascend, then it's not a switchback. If while taking a step you dislodge a rock and it rolls down the trail like a runaway snowball in the Alps, then you're not hiking on switchbacks. Forget the hiking guidebooks; there are no switchbacks on the trail between Lower Yosemite Falls and Upper Yosemite Falls.

There is only pain, sweat, and agony. Such was our trip along this portion of the trail. We continued up the trail, taking ten steps and resting for fifteen seconds, ten steps, rest for fifteen seconds, and so on. Although we were moving very slowly, no one was passing us even though we did see people at the bottom of the falls that day. So, we thought, maybe we were not doing too badly after all. Perhaps the hike up the falls is just that difficult. Then we were smacked by reality in the form of Steve Austin and Jamie Sommers.

In the seventies, there was a television series called the "Six Million Dollar Man" starring Steve Austin; an astronaut that was involved in a plane crash and the only way to save him was to replace some of his human components with bionics, making him The Bionic Man. Steve's love interest was Jamie Sommers, who oddly enough was involved in a car crash and needed bionics to be saved, thus making her The Bionic Woman. Now although these characters were from a fictional television series that aired over thirty years ago, we were about to meet the real bionic man and bionic woman.

At some point during the hike up Upper Yosemite Falls, I don't know when exactly as I was delirious from the pain and the heat, we heard a couple approaching from below us. We did not hear them because of the noise their feet were making, we heard them talking. We turned and were astonished to see that they weren't hiking up the trail, they were running up the trail and they weren't talking, they were arguing! Here we were, plodding along like pachyderms, ten steps, rest for fifteen seconds, and they were running and arguing. They had to be bionic. It is the only explanation. How else could they run up the trail that was clearly kicking our asses, and still have enough energy left to argue? When I argue with my wife, it takes everything I have. If I tried to do something else while arguing, I would surely lose focus, and the next thing I know, I would be apologizing for something that may or may not have been my fault. Arguing with your spouse is exhausting enough without adding running up a mountain. Yet here they were, running by us and:

"Why didn't you call first?" (Jamie)

"I didn't think it would be that big of a deal." (Steve)

"Not that big of a deal, you know I don't like people just showing up. You know I need notice so I can straighten up." (Jamie)

"Straighten up, you're always straightening up." (Steve)

They passed us and their voices faded as they continued to run up the trough that is the Upper Yosemite Falls trail. It almost broke my spirit. I came close to sitting right in the trail until I had the strength to retreat to the comfort of my truck. But after laughing hysterically for at least sixty seconds, or maybe I was crying, you'll have to ask James, I composed myself and up we continued.

At the point of complete exhaustion, we reached the top of Yosemite Falls which features a breathtaking overlook of the Valley called "Yosemite Point." The view was, as many in Yosemite are, indescribable in these pages. But we had work to do. It was one in the afternoon. A decision needed to be made; do we continue on to North Dome, which was still five miles away, or do we rest and go back the way we came. Since the guidebook we use to plan our trips clearly and unequivocally states, and I quote, "If you are exhausted when you reach Yosemite Point, turn back", our choice was made for us. We continued on to North Dome. In our world, the world of two schmucks, confidence and stupidity are synonymous.

The view from the top of Yosemite Falls is spectacular. As you look over the valley, El Capitan is on your right and Half Dome is on your left. Across the valley is Bridalveil Falls. In April and May, the view is probably even more impressive as Yosemite Falls would be plummeting three-quarters of a mile to the valley floor. Each person will have to decide for themselves if the view is worth the hike, but for me, the view coupled with the fact that the worst part of the hike was behind us, made for a wonderful moment at the top of Yosemite Falls. A wonderful moment created in part, by the abject delusion that the worst part of the hike was behind us. The worst part of the hike lay far ahead of us.

Yosemite Falls is not the highest point on the North Dome hike. I'm not even sure if North Dome is the highest point. Just beyond Yosemite Falls is a small granite dome that to the best of my knowledge has no name and may be the highest point of the hike. We scampered up the dome with no-name and had lunch. Since we had reached the high point of the hike, or at the very least, close to the high point, and since we were approximately half-way through the hike, we felt North Dome was easily within our reach. We had completely forgotten about the Fundamental Law of Backpacking. Schmucks.

Laws Cannot Be Broken

After lunch, we continued our hike to North Dome by descending the dome with no-name. As Rule Number 3 states, since we were descending, we would be ascending very shortly; and so, we did. We descended from the dome with no-name and ascended up the hill of trees and then descended the hill with trees and ascended the hill with more trees then descended the hill with more trees and ascended the hill with trees and a stream and then…. I think you know where this is going. Up and down we went, using whatever leg muscles you use to climb and then using whatever leg muscles you use to descend. Up, down, ascend, descend, elevation gain, elevation loss. If you believe that "whatever the Lord giveth, the Lord taketh away", then the Lord was in a very giving and taking mood that day.

At some point during this real-world proof of the Fundamental Law of Backpacking, James and I had switched positions. James was now leading and slowing pulling away from me. I think James had a little bit of Steve Austin in him because he was not only leaving me behind, he was carrying cans of Hormel Stew and Chili as well as the canister from Mordor and leaving me behind.

I'm guessing we were over six miles in of our seven-and-a-half-mile hike, when I shouted out to James, "Hey! If we go up one more time, I'm done. That's it! I'm pitching my tent wherever we're at. I'm not going any further."

James turned and shouted back, "It only goes up, like, a little."

A little! Lying bastard. Damn him and his second wind….

I stopped dead in my tracks and urged James to go on without me. Being the good friend and wingman that he is, of course, did not go on without me. He laughed at me; then waited until I realized that I had to press on and together we climbed the next hill with trees.

During the hike up Yosemite Falls, you can see North Dome. Once you leave the dome with no-name, you lose sight of North Dome and you pick it up again during the final half mile of the hike. When we broke from the trees and beheld the granite out-cropping that was our goal, confidence filled my being and pushed me on. Of course, though, the final half mile was no different than the previous three. After breaking from the woods, we scrambled down a granite hillside, clinging to the rock wall on our left, choosing our steps carefully as not to sprain an ankle this close to our goal and this far from my truck. After reaching the bottom of the granite hill, you ascend through the woods of North Dome, finally emerging at the granite outcropping. Where the woods meet the granite is a perfect place to camp. There we dropped our backs and strolled, yes strolled, the final 100 yards to the top of North Dome.

North Dome

If the view from the top of Yosemite Falls is spectacular. words simply can't describe the view from North Dome; El Capitan and the Cathedral Rocks frame the entrance to Yosemite Valley, you can see the Three Brothers, Sentinel Rock, Sentinel Dome, and Clouds Rest dominates the east side, as the Merced River winds its way through the valley some 7500 feet below. And, right in front of you is the sheer face of Half Dome. In the spirit of full disclosure, the only features previously mentioned that I can pick out with any confidence is Half Dome, El Capitan, and the Merced River. There is no doubt in my mind that the other features are there; I'm just not talented enough to distinguish one granite outcropping from another.

James and I stood on North Dome as the sun went down posing like Rocky on the steps of the Philadelphia Art Museum. In only our second backpacking trip, we had reached our destination. After failing so badly on our last trip, this success was immeasurable. We had reached the top of North Dome, via Yosemite Falls, while wearing shoes used for hiking shopping malls and carrying a bear canister whose use, we have yet to determine.

We pitched our tents around 4:30pm, as the sun was setting behind Half Dome. Due to the infrequency of backpackers at North Dome, there was plenty of firewood. We started our fire; well, that sounds too easy.

In actuality, we attempted to start a fire. For whatever reason, when you have pine needles, small twigs, paper and matches you do not have what you need to start a fire. If you did, then we would have had no issues with the fire. But that wasn't the case. Match after match went into the small pile of fire ingredients, but no flames issued forth. This is extremely odd considering that every year someone driving at 60 mph throws a smoldering cigarette butt from their car and ignites a raging blaze that engulfs 3000 acres. We were trying to intentionally start a fire, using fire, and could not burn two handfuls of brush. After this frustration at North Dome, and a few more frustrating nights (because schmucks don't learn lessons easily), fire paste became a staple of our backpacking equipment.

In the end, the fire got going and we settled in for dinner followed by bragging about the day's hike. Unlike Alder Creek, the night sky was clear and we were able to cook under the stars. Unfortunately, that did not change the fact that freeze-dried food comes out partially cooked. I ended up drinking half my mac-n-cheese and crunching the other half. James' stew was much better but not worth the extra effort of hauling each can to the top of North Dome. After dinner, we each had some hot chocolate, which will always lift your spirits on a cool night. We finished dinner and stuffed all items with a scent into the bear canister. This time, James' had the strength necessary to throw the canister a good 10 feet from the campsite. Of course, James walked over, picked up the canister and walked it at least 100 feet from the campsite. It was in the mid 40's by the time we turned in, not even close to my sleeping bag rating of 20 degrees.

There was no rain that night, no snow, no ice, no falling tree. Still, I didn't sleep well. When you're exhausted from the day's hike, you go to sleep quickly. Staying asleep is quite another matter. I had a small sleeping mat under my sleeping bag. The mat is supposed to serve two purposes; provide insulation from the coldness of the ground and provide a cushion from the hardness of the ground. It fails on both counts. Luckily my sleeping bag protected me from the cold but did nothing to protect me from the ground. Every few minutes I was awaked by tingling in whichever arm I happened to be lying upon. I would roll over, drift back off and then be awakened again. This went on for the entirety of the night. Not complaining though – I actually awoke well rested and ready to begin the trek back to the valley floor.

James climbed out of his tent after the fire was going and stated that all-in-all he slept pretty well. His sleeping mat consisted of a small air pad and by his account, it provided the comfort necessary to get a good night's sleep. I was happy for James. After all, he was able to walk the trail faster than me, was able to get a good night's sleep and arose to a warming fire that I created in the cold. I thought, good for James; after all, he'll need the rest since he'll be hauling that godforsaken bear canister back down the mountain. He should have a good sleep and warm fire the son-of-a-….

I made some hot chocolate, James made coffee and we headed to the top of North Dome to watch the sun rise over the valley. First, the sun lit up the face of El Capitan and then sparkled off the waters of the Merced River. The sun then chased the shadows from North Dome, warmed our faces and shined off the sheer cliff of Half Dome. It was a great sunrise, only made better by the deer standing behind us. For the next few moments that morning, deer were crossing North Dome between us and our campsite. We sat there in silence, watching the sunrise and deer crossing North Dome.

But all good things must end and this moment in time was no exception. So, we picked ourselves up, went back to the campsite, packed up the gear, put out the fire, and headed down to the valley, back the way we came.

A New Rule

We hiked down through the woods of North Dome, scrambled up the granite hill, holding on to the side as not to slide to certain injury and began ascending and descending and ascending and descending and so on and so on through hills covered in trees. Returning through this portion of the trail was much easier than arriving. We were not already exhausted from the climb up Yosemite Falls, so although the giving and taking of elevation took its toll, it did not beat me to the point of yelling out that I quit. That would come later.

We reached the dome with no-name somewhere around noon but didn't stop for lunch. We never stop for lunch on the return trip as we want to save our appetite for the pizza or the Big Mac that awaits us in whatever town we pass through on our way back to Fresno. Some men celebrate a day's accomplishment with a cold brew; we celebrate with a large pizza and a vat of Mountain Dew or a Big Mac and a supersized Coke. I could be wrong but I don't think our diet improves our ability to backpack.

We scampered down the dome with no-name and dropped on the top of Yosemite Falls. Our legs were tired but we could see the end. We knew we would be down in about thirty minutes. Our spirits were high as we started down Yosemite Falls. Our spirits crashed and burned about ten minutes later. It is then that we learned the Fourth Rule of Backpacking: *the time it takes and the pain you feel going up a hill or mountain will be at least even to the time it takes and pain you feel going down the same hill or mountain.* This rule may not be evident when going up and down hills with an elevation of a couple hundred feet, but this rule will smack you in the face when descending Yosemite Falls.

Ten minutes into the descent my knees were shot. It was so steep that I was walking stiff-legged, almost falling from step to step. Every step was met with a bone-jarring thud of my knees and ankles. My shoes, the ones sewed by the Devil's Cobblers, provided no ankle support; so, each step on rock or step would turn my ankle to the right and then the left. Going up Yosemite Falls we had to stop every ten paces to catch our breath. Going down Yosemite Falls we had to stop every ten paces to allow the pain in our knees and or ankles to subside. Ten minutes into a three-and-a-half-hour descent, we realized this was going to be brutal.

On and on we went, down Yosemite Falls. Step by step, thud by thud. You could hear the knees screaming in pain. You could feel the ankles twisting this way than that. Going forward was inconceivable; going back was not an option. Luckily gravity made our decision easy and so we continued to descend.

After a couple of hours, we were in the switchbacks of Lower Yosemite Falls. Unfortunately, the switchbacks provided no relief. The switchbacks of Lower Yosemite Falls are not smooth, tree-lined, dirt trails. No sir, those switchbacks are rock studded and root covered. It is rare to find a smooth spot large enough to fit your foot. So once again the ankles were twisting and the knees were crashing. The real tragedy is that all the switchbacks looked the same and you could never see the bottom. So, every time you completed a switchback you knew that it was the last switchback; which of course it was not, in fact, there were another hundred or so of the switchbacks still to complete. Our confidence would rise and be dashed, rise and be dashed; our ankles were twisting left and right, left and right, and our knees were crashing and crashing and crashing. So, it continued down Yosemite Falls.

About half-way down the switchbacks of Lower Yosemite Falls, we met a couple of Scandinavian families heading up to Lower Yosemite Falls; two women, two men, and about four children. We assumed they were Scandinavian by their accents and the fact that all the family members were blonde-haired and blue-eyed. We stopped the women; of course, we stopped the women, after all, they were blonde-haired, blue-eyed, Scandinavian women, and asked them how far to the bottom. Now just so no one thinks we were using our misery to hit on these Nordic beauties, we stopped and asked everyone we had seen that day how much further to the bottom. What made this situation different is these women asked us how far to the top! We told them it was 3.5 miles from the bottom to the top of Yosemite Falls and about a 3600-foot elevation gain. We also told them that there was no water anywhere along the trail including at the top of the trail so they needed to be carrying plenty of water. They showed us the two small bottles of water they were carrying and we promptly warned them that they would die. This, of course, shocked the women and caused the children to panic. The men, on the other hand, would not be deterred and simply stated that they could make the top of the falls because they were doctors. I, of course, am not a doctor. I am also certain that James is not a doctor. However, I believe what makes a doctor successful is their access to items that would help in a medical situation, such as bandages, medicine, splints, and in this case, water. In this situation though, the Scandinavian doctors did not have access to any of the aforementioned life-saving inventories. So, we left the doctors heading up the falls, the children following behind, and the women standing, staring at us in disbelief with their mouths agape. There is no doubt in my mind that those families turned back that day somewhere along the basin of Lower Yosemite Falls.

We, however, continued on down the trail. Stopping every few paces to rest our joints and ask passersby, "how much further." All the answers were the same, "just a few more switchbacks" which roughly translated in trail lingo is: "if you have to ask, you're gonna die." Finally, to our amazement, we stepped off the last switchback and onto a short steep trail that marked the beginning of our adventure just the day before. We were at the base of Yosemite Falls and the only thing that stood between us and my truck was the three-quarter mile hike across the valley floor. I think I openly wept when I realized I wasn't done walking.

James had a great idea to limit our pain of hiking across the valley. He suggested we take the shuttle around the valley. Yes, it would make the trip longer, but we would be sitting and not walking. What a brilliant idea; that is, until we had to stand again.

Carol Comes to our Rescue

We caught the shuttle a mere hundred yards from the trailhead, pushed ourselves to the back of the shuttle and dropped down on a couple empty seats.

As we made our way to the back of the shuttle, we received many an interesting stare. I don't know if the other passengers felt sorry for us because we looked so disheveled, or if they felt for us because they could see the pain in our eyes, or if they felt for me because they could see I obviously sucked at choosing footwear or if they just could not stand the foul, backcountry stench that must have been emanating from our bodies. After all, we did spend two days hiking up and down Yosemite Falls with backpacks in temperatures that regularly reached the 80's. Whichever the reason, the stares we received that day certainly made me feel self-conscience; but nothing was going to make me get off of that shuttle until we reached our parking lot. A fact that would soon be tested.

Fifteen minutes on the shuttle and we were coming to the bus stop near my truck's parking lot. As we neared the bus stop, I made my way to the front of the shuttle and asked Bus Driver Carol, as all female bus drivers are named "Carol," if she could take us to the parking lot, to which she replied, "No". Obviously, she saw our desperation at having to walk again, ever. Finally, should took pity upon us and drove to the parking lot where my truck was waiting to take us to our victory meal. Carol took us to the parking lot even though not five minutes earlier she said, "No, the bus can only go from bus stop to bus stop, no exceptions." But she was making an exception for us. Bus Driver Carol was making an exception because she knew I could not make the quarter-mile walk from the bus stop to the parking lot. She saw it in my eyes. She knew the trail beat me like I'm sure it beat so many before me. Bus Driver Carol knew that if she dropped us at the bus stop, I would sit there and cry; probably spend the night there. Bus Driver Carol was correct.

So, thanks to Bus Driver Carol and our own pure determination and will, we didn't have to spend another night in Yosemite. We made it to my truck around three in the afternoon, dropped our packs in the bed, dropped the bear canister at the Ranger Station (for the last time) and headed out of Yosemite National Park.

Victory Comes at a Price

North Dome via Yosemite Falls backpacking trip did not end that Sunday when we climbed into the truck. It did not end when we arrived back in Fresno. The North Dome via Yosemite Falls backpacking trip did not end for at least two weeks after we left the trail that Sunday.

For a full week after the North Dome trip, I could not make it up the stairs in my house; I could not climb in and out of my truck, hell I could barely walk. Each morning I awoke, my ankles and knees were so stiff that I could only stand in one place. If I tried to move too fast, I would fall and lay on the floor until my wife came to my aid. If I stayed stationary too long, my ankles and knees would freeze again and I would need assistance to get moving. Little by little though, day by day, my joints would loosen and by the beginning of the second week I was almost back to normal. Conversations with James during my week in convalescence convinced me that he was no better off than I.

We had been victorious, but it came at a price. A price I would gladly pay again if it meant taking on Mother Nature, taking on our own stupidity, pushing past our shortcomings, and reaching our stated objective. After all, how do we know what we're capable of until we test ourselves and in doing so, reach our limit; a limit that we still have not reached because we were victorious.

Winter Hits the Sierra Nevadas

Let It Snow, Let It Snow, Let It Snow…

Although we were victorious at North Dome, we couldn't help but imagine what we could have accomplished if we would have incorporated all the lessons learned at Alder Creek and actually paid attention to our own rules.

For those that like to keep track, we now had Four Rules:

1. *It's All in the Shoes*
2. *Lighter is Better*
3. *Fundamental Law of Backpacking – What Goes Down, Must Go Up*
4. *The time it takes and the pain you feel going up a hill or mountain will be at least even to the time it takes and pain you feel going down the same hill or mountain*

one good idea – know the weather of your destination, one truism – when one suffers all suffer, and Vito's Maxim - the feeling of joy that comes with the completion of an adventure is directly proportional with the adversities that must be overcome during said adventure. We had agreed that on our next backpacking trip we would incorporate all the aforementioned knowledge. Unfortunately, we thought we might have to wait a few months for it was winter in the Sierra Nevadas.

There are no rules or laws prohibiting backpacking in the Sierra Nevadas during winter. In fact, the three major parks near Fresno, Yosemite, Kings Canyon, and Sequoia, are open year-round. So, we were planning on backpacking right through the winter snows. We thought it would be awesome to hike all day through the cool, crisp air, over the white snow. We wouldn't have to fight through the thorny manzanita groves or worry about losing the trail over a granite dome. We would simply head out cross-country and then follow our trail back the way we came. At the end of the hiking day, we would dig down in the snow and set-up our tents, then sit around the warm fire and….

wait.... there may be a flaw in our plan. Fire needs wood and snow covers wood; therefore, snow cancels fire and no fire equals no backpacking; a kind of backpacking Ro-Sham-Bo.

One of the things James and I enjoy most about backpacking is sitting around the warm fire, reflecting on the day's events and contemplating what the future might hold. Without a fire, you're just sitting in the dark talking to each other. You know what they call sitting in the dark talking to each other? A séance. I'm not having a séance in the middle of the woods. Newspaper articles start that way. Headline: Hikers Mauled by Conjured Wendigo in Snow Covered Forest. No thanks. My imagination can create enough characters and scenarios to freak me out without throwing a séance in the mix. Bottom line, if I'm going to spend a night in the woods, I want a fire.

We Head South

Just because there's snow in the Sierra Nevadas doesn't mean there's snow everywhere. We just needed to hike in lower elevations or find a place where snow is a rarity, even in higher elevations. We needed to head south to Southern California and the Angeles National Forest.

Just north of Los Angeles is the Angeles National Forest situated in the famous San Gabriel Mountains. Although there are snow-covered peaks above 10,000 feet, most of the Angeles National Forest is below 7,000 feet and therefore snow-free; perfect for backpackers wanting to backpack during the winter months but still wanting to enjoy a warm fire during the evening. So, in January, we headed south to the Angeles National Forest to a place named Devil's Canyon Trail. Our policies against holding séances has already paid off...

Difference Makers

This trip, however, was going to be completely different than our first two trips, and not just because my wife was coming. Yes. – My wife accompanied us on this trip. We thought since the first two trips were so successful, we needed to introduce another variable into the backpacking equation; something that would be as unpredictable as the weather or the trail itself. Certainly, a woman would fit the bill perfectly. Not just any woman though. We needed a menopausal-arachnophobia. This trip needed my wife. Now you may think I'm pushing the boundaries of political correctness and sexism. But my wife was menopausal, is afraid of spiders, and as any good chauvinist will tell you, women are occasionally unpredictable.

Now it wasn't my wife that made this trip completely different; okay, it wasn't <u>only</u> my wife that made this trip completely different than our first two trips; it was the fact that we were going to follow the Rules of Backpacking and all other lessons learned. To that end, I shit-canned my Trailgear shoes. No more was I going to haul those pounds of leather blocks up and down the mountain. No more was I going to torture my toes and allow my ankles to snap back and forth like some turn of the century marionette. I purchased me a proper set of backpacking shoes from, let the choir sing out, "AHHHHH", REI!! I purchased a pair of Montrail backpacking shoes with Vibram® soles and Gore-Tex® uppers, size 15, medium width, waterproof, weighing in at a scant 4.0 pounds, for the pair! I don't know if Montrail still makes backpacking shoes, I know they make running shoes, but when I bought these backpacking shoes, they were the bomb. My feet, which James calls pontoons, still love me for it.

You may think I'm going too far when talking about the shoes, but I'm telling you, you can't go too far when it comes to backpacking shoes. I could write 10 pages about the shoes alone and it wouldn't be too far. I could hold a seminar about backpacking footwear and it still wouldn't be too far. I could get one gift a year if it was backpacking shoes, and that wouldn't be too far. I could have erotic dreams that included backpacking shoes and that ……okay, that would be too far. But the other things would not. My Vibram® soles held me steady when I rock hopped across the streams of Last Chance Camp and they clung to the slick rock of the dried waterfalls of Flat Iron. The Gore-Tex® uppers held my ankles in check as I bounded down Chilnualna Trail and slipped and slid up the scrabble of Alta Peak. My Montrails kept my feet dry through the November snows in Yosemite Valley and the shallow streams of Panther Creek.

I'm telling you, you want to go backpacking or hiking, you even thinking about going backpacking or hiking; the first step – get the right shoes. The right shoes will make all the difference in the world. And now, I had the right shoes.

Along with the perfect footwear, I had the perfect dinner. Gone were the freeze-dried meals that would inevitably end in half soupy-half uncooked, always disappointing dinner. In their place, I had the college student's staple, and now Two-Schmucks Officially Trail-Rated Ramen Noodles. It was actually my wife's idea and what a great idea it was! Hey, I give credit where credit is due. They come in self-contained single serving bowls and all you add is hot water. It just occurred to me, that sounds like a freeze-dried meal. But it can't be because Ramen Noodles come out perfect every time. So, I don't care if they sound like freeze-dried meals or not, Ramen Noodles are perfect for backpacking. Although the fact that they are packaged in Styrofoam does mean that they can get easily damaged. I guess there's always room for improvement. James also went with the backpacker's delight known as Ramen Noodles in lieu of his stake-pounding cans of Hormel products.

The last thing to be replaced was the bear canister. We replaced the bear canister with …… nothing at all. I don't know if bear canisters are required in Angeles National Forest, I don't know if there are even bears in the Angeles, but we didn't care. After Alder Creek and North Dome, we were not hauling, or more correctly, James was not hauling another bear canister. We would stuff all items with a scent in a sack and toss the sack off into the distance; maybe even bury the sack. If a bear came across the sack and developed an affection for the great taste of hot chocolate, or Ramen Noodles, or toothpaste, then so be it. That was a bullet we would have to take. We, James, was not hauling another bear canister.

Perfect shoes, great dinner, no more bear canister – now I needed to outfit my wife. Another reason to go to REI. Life was good.

Jo got herself a backpack, a 15-degree sleeping bag (should have got the 0-degree bag) and a great pair of backpacking shoes. I never knew if my wife would go backpacking again, but I was not putting her feet through the hell mine experienced, not even one time. She did not get her own tent. In the past, I have stated that there is no way two men can fit into a two-man backpacking tent, but a man and a woman is another story, and a fun one at that! Yet, again I digress. My two-man tent would be just fine for me and my wife.

"Left Turn Clyde"

Devil's Canyon, in the Angeles National Forest, is approximately four hours from Fresno; just north of La Canada-Flintridge on Hwy 2. If you don't know where La Canada-Flintridge is, just think Los Angeles. There are dozens of communities surrounding Los Angeles. If we were in New York they would be called boroughs and if we were in Chicago, they would be called suburbs, but in Los Angeles, they're called communities and La Canada-Flintridge is one such community. Since James lives in the high desert of Southern California, he was going to meet us at the trailhead.

Jo and I took off around five in the morning on a Saturday in January. January in Fresno means lows in the 40's and highs in the 60's. That morning was no different and by the time we reached the trailhead the temperature was in the mid 50's on its way to a gorgeous 75° day.

We reached the trailhead just before nine and James pulled in just past nine. On the right side of the parking lot was the trail down to Devil's Canyon. On the left side of the parking lot were some unnamed trails that led up into the hills. Our plan was to take the trail down to Devil's Canyon. A good plan too, until Boy Scouts Troop 18 pulled into the parking lot.

Most people, many people, would have had no issue hiking the same trail as Boy Scouts Troop 18. After all, according to the Troop Master, or Scout Master, or Ring Master, or whatever you call the semi-creepy person that leads the Boy Scouts, there was plenty of camping spots in Devil's Canyon and the Boy Scouts would be happy to share their camping areas. James and I, on the other hand, wanted nothing to do with Boy Scouts Troop 18. Troop 18 should not take it personally, as we had nothing personal against the troop or even Boy Scouts in general. We just don't like people.

To date, I've stated three reasons why we like to go backpacking; sitting around the fire at night, challenge ourselves – push ourselves to the limit, and to get away from people. Hiking with Boy Scouts Troop 18 would not be getting away from people. In fact, it would be the exact opposite. If I'm going to hike with Boy Scouts Troop 18, I might as well drive south a few miles and hike in the Glendale Galleria Mall.

Needless to say, we did not head right out of the parking lot. We headed left to the unnamed trails that led up into the hills of the Angeles National Forest.

At this point, our trip might sound like a lead-in to a movie containing hill folk, incestuous relations and someone fond of human skin; a movie entitled "Right Turn Only" or "No Left Turn". Believe me, we had some of the same thoughts as we started out with no map and no idea where the trails would take us. But rest assured, we met none of the aforementioned characters. We actually had, by all accounts, a very nice hike.

I know I made fun of my wife a few paragraphs earlier, but she is an avid walker and hiker. We spent many an afternoon hiking the trails of Yosemite, Kings Canyon, and Sequoia. She had no issues with her backpack or the trails. These trails were modest and we took many breaks in order to determine where we were and where we were going. It was a great morning and a great afternoon. The evening, on the other hand, could have been better.

Mid 40's

We happened upon a campground in the late afternoon, perhaps 3:30. It wasn't a backpacker's camping area, it was actually a drive-in campground. I couldn't tell you where the entrance was but probably somewhere off of HWY 2. My guess is we hiked away from the highway and then through all our twists and turns headed back towards the same highway, or the highway was twisting and turning the whole time we were twisting and turning and we were never more than a couple miles from the highway. In either case, at around 3:30 we came around a ridge and there was Horse Back Camp. I wouldn't swear that Horse Back Camp was the name of the campground, but it was to the best of my recollection.

The campground was empty, perfect for James and me, and consisted of a dozen or more campsites and at least one out-house, perfect for Jo. We pitched our tents in a campsite next to a small running creek (remember I said "running"). We gathered up a night's supply of wood (what we thought would last the night, anyway) and then settled in for an evening of contemplation and reflection.

At the time we were setting up camp, the temperature was in the low 70's or high 60's. As the sun went down, so did the temperature. I don't know what time it was when we first realized it was cold. It might have been when I left the fire to relieve myself or when my wife left the fire to relieve herself. Either way, it was cold when you left the fire. But hey, we were in Southern California so it could not have been that cold, probably in the mid-40's.

The cold wasn't the only thing that came upon us as the sun went down; we were also visited by the youth of La Canada. Instantly, I started thinking about hill folks. Remember, my imagination can freak me out sometimes.

In the dark, a few, 2 or 3 or 4, pick-ups rolled in with what we ascertained as young ne'er do wells from the foothill community of La Canada-Flintridge. Perhaps Horse Back is known as the Saturday night

55

party spot or perhaps these were just some teens returning from a day of snow-skiing. Either way, once the pick-ups rolled in, the fire started burning, the music started playing and the beer, I'm guessing beer by the sound of the pull tabs, started pouring.

The youth of La Canada, clearly in need of effective parenting, stayed for a couple hours and that wasn't too bad. The music was good and it helped keep our minds off the cold, which by now was still in the mid-40's. Before we turned in, the youth had returned from whence they came.

By the time we turned in, it was pretty damn cold; probably in the mid-40's. My wife was the first to realize that the fire was not going to be enough to ward off the coldness so she turned in first, followed by me (the dutiful husband), and then James.

When I climbed in the tent, Jo was already snuggled up in her sleeping bag and I dove into mine. She was awake and asked me what I thought was the temperature, to which I replied, "Mid 40's", of course. That's the last of the conversation I remember until I heard this awful chattering noise. It sounded like Chatterer, Pinhead's cenobite partner in the movie *Hellraiser*. First the hill people and then Chatterer, I was freaking out until I realized that the cenobite was my wife!

I heard the saying that it's so cold it will make your teeth chatter, but I never witnessed the phenomenon, until that evening. Jo's teeth were chattering so hard that the sound woke me from my slumber. She was shivering as if she just climbed out of Lake Michigan on a February morning. I couldn't believe it and worse, at first, I didn't know what to do. I tried to comfort her and rub her to warm her up, the whole time consoling her with the fact that it wasn't that cold. She was in a 15° bag and it was in the mid-40's. Jo would have none of it. She was freezing and needed warmth immediately. Jo climbed into my sleeping bag.

You may think I'm exaggerating when I talk about how small a two-man backpacking tent is, but there is no way I'm exaggerating when I tell you that a single person sleeping bag is made for one person; unless of course the other person is your half-frozen wife. Somehow, we got her into my sleeping bag and zipped it completely. The only thing protruding from my sleeping bag was our noses. Without that little airhole, we would have died that night from carbon-dioxide poisoning. But with that bag zipped up, there was no more shivering and no more teeth chattering. The warmest place that night in Angeles National Forest was inside my sleeping bag with me and my wife.

Unfortunately, the next morning she woke with a splitting migraine. For all you migraine sufferers, you know how debilitating a migraine can be and she was facing a hike out of the backcountry with one such debilitating migraine. Luckily, she packed Imetrix®, so with some water and a little time, the migraine would be extinguished and we could head back to civilization.

There was only one problem with that plan, we had no water. We arrived in camp with water and camped next to a running creek, so we should have plenty of water, but we did not. What we did have was plenty of ice! All the water in our hydration packs froze. All the water in our bottles froze. All the water in the running creek froze. Turns out, during the night it got slightly colder than the mid-40's. In reality, it got down to 17°. My wife no longer relies on me for temperature estimates.

As close as Schmuck I would get to his wife once she found out it was 17° the night before

After we regained our composure from laughing at the fact that our water had frozen during the night, James started the fire, we melted the ice back into water, Jo took her Imetrix®, we had breakfast, packed up our gear, and hiked back the way we came, out of the Angeles National Forest.

Angeles Too Cold

We Head West

Jo didn't want to accompany us on our February backpacking trip. She said she didn't want to interfere with our bromance, but I think she was still recovering from her near Popsicle experience. I was okay with her sitting this one out. Not because I needed special time with James, but because when it's just James and me, our trips tend to be a little more adventurous and by adventurous, I mean treacherous and dangerous. February's trip to Last Chance Camp in the Los Padres National Forest would certainly prove this point.

Last Chance Camp wasn't our first choice for February. I don't even know if it was a conscious choice or a place we just happened upon. Our first choice was Big Sur. It's on the coast, low elevation and certainly doesn't see any snow, or 17° temperatures. Unfortunately, during that winter, Big Sur wasn't seeing any campfires either. Due to the major drought that winter, many areas had fire restrictions and Big Sur was one of them. You know how I feel about camping without fire so needless to say, we did not go to Big Sur. Instead, we chose Arroyo Seco, which of course, did not happen.

Los Padres is three to four hours from Fresno, depending on which area of the forest you're visiting, so we left about six in the morning. We were in high spirits because we finally had all the proper equipment, from the shoes to the tents to the food. However, on this trip, James would teach me one more lesson. As stated earlier, there is always room for improvement.

As we entered the National Forest we came upon the ubiquitous welcome shack where you pay your entrance fee. This shack was different from most as it hasn't changed since the 49ers came looking for gold. Ma and Pa Kettle came out of their house to collect the entrance fee. When I say "house," I literally mean a house as the shack was in their front yard. The fee to enter was $7, cash only; proof that the shack's been there since the gold rush. James nor I had $7 cash as cash doesn't come in handy in the wilderness. I mean I've never tried, but I don't think you can pay-off a bear; not with cash anyhow. We did have our National Parks pass and debit cards which of course were as useless as my Trailgear hiking shoes. We also had our charm and natural good looks, which it turns out, are worth about $7, because after some smooth talking, Ma and Pa Kettle, mainly Ma Kettle, let us in the park provided we promised to mail a check for $7. Which, upon returning to Fresno, we promptly did.

Once we negotiated our way into the National Forest, we pulled into the Arroyo Seco area and determined rather quickly that Arroyo Seco wasn't for us. It was too short of a hike and seemed to have too many people on the trail. Luckily, we had a Los Padres map and chose a new destination, Last Chance Camp.

Omen of Things to Come

The trail went downhill from the parking lot, which of course seems like a good thing until you remember the fundamental law; although the elevation gains were not the real issue that day. Once we hit the bottom of the hill we were in a valley and the hike leveled off nicely. Within the first mile we came upon a stream or small river, depending on when you're telling this story. If you're telling this story in the middle of the day, relatively sober, among family, it was a stream. If you're telling this story in the evening, around a fire, after a few beers with friends, it was a raging river. Either way, the water was about calf deep, so wading across was not appealing. Luckily there were some large rocks which would allow for boulder hopping.

Generally speaking, I lead the way when we go hiking. No special reason, just the way things have played out. So, I was the first to boulder hop across the river; river in this case because it makes the events sound more ominous and less embarrassing. It is not easy to boulder hop with 35 pounds on your back, although the gripping power of my shoes certainly helped off-set my lack of stability, I was able to make it across without getting wet.

Once on the other side, I asked James to wait until I got my camera ready. Although I didn't foresee James falling in the river, I certainly did not want to miss out on a YouTube moment should he happen to fall in the river, and being the good and thoughtful partner, that James is, he did not let my camera preparation go to waste.

I don't know if James even made it off the first rock before dropping calf-deep in the water, but I know he went in early during his boulder hopping, or more exact, his failure at boulder hopping. What made it even better is that he thought he could salvage his dignity by stepping on the next boulder and then resuming the hopping; which of course was a complete failure as once again off the boulder he went and back into the river. James was then kind enough to complete this cycle one more time. I now have three perfect pictures of James' calf-deep in water, cold February mountain water, while not six inches away, rise perfectly dry boulders large enough for my size 15 feet to stand upon. James, and in his usual manner, would prove to be the comic relief on this trip. Schmuck.

Once he was safe across the river, albeit with cold, wet feet, we resumed our hike and within a mile reached what would be our backpacking defining moment. One might think our backpacking defining moment already occurred, what with the Battle at Alder Creek. Although that trip certainly helped define how we would handle adversity in the backcountry, there was no real choice made at Alder Creek as we were already in the shit. Therefore, we had no real choice except to push through. Here, on the other hand, we had a choice as we stood on the trail to Last Chance Camp in the Los Padres National Forest, at around 9 a.m. in February, James with soaked, wet feet, reading the sign in front of us; "Abandoned Trail. Do Not Proceed Past this Point".

Two questions immediately came to mind:

1) do we really want to turn around and,

2) what does "Abandoned" mean?

The answer to the first question was easy, "no", and probably drove us to rationalize the answer to the second question. Does "Abandoned" mean that the trail is no longer maintained, someone hiking the trail on a regular basis picking up limbs, sawing trees, that kind of thing, or does "Abandoned" mean that a new, easier trail has been cut through the mountains and therefore, why use this trail? Regardless of the answer, an abandoned trail doesn't sound like a real problem especially given the fact that we weren't going to turn around. So off we went in an effort to define the meaning to "Abandoned Trail"; which in this case meant "Trail Under Water"!

Within a couple miles of James' River, we came upon another river, at least we thought it was a river, and we needed to boulder hop again. I, of course, made it across with no issues and James, of course, spent as much time in the river as possible. Once on the other side of the "river", the trail ended. There was no trail and nothing that was even discernible as remnants of a trail. There were only rocks and logs and twigs and ribbons; bright pink ribbons tied in the trees. The ribbons were the markers of the trail. The trail itself has washed away and/or buried under debris and when I say washed away, what I mean is, the trail was underwater.

The valley, where the trail once was, before it was abandoned, was now under water and the only way to proceed was to either crisscross the river using boulders or wade through the river. We chose to boulder hop our way through the valley, although James could have just waded through the river given the time he spent in the water.

I'm not exaggerating when I say we must have crisscrossed that river a half dozen times and James must have fallen off boulders and into the river a dozen times. By the end, James ignored the rocks all together and just walked through the water.

Be Careful What You Wish For

After a mile or so, a mile as the crow flies and two miles as we were crisscrossing, the trail made its way up the hillside, leaving the river behind. Once we were about half way up the hill, the trail leveled off again. Over the next few miles, the trail would be in the warm, glowing sun and then wrap around the hill and cross into the cool shade before crossing to the next hill and emerging back into the sunlight and then receding back into the shade. There were some spectacular views when the trail was cut into the side of the hills. The valley extended to your left and right and the river shimmered some 1,500 feet below. This was a great part of the hike and we were happy to be out of the river, ignorant to what lay ahead.

At approximately the three-quarter point of our hike, about five miles in, while walking in the sunlight some 1,500 feet above the river, the trail once again came to an end. This time the trail wasn't underwater, it was under about eight feet of debris. A rock slide had wiped out the trail. We were done. No more hiking except the hiking that would be involved in going back the way we came; back through the river. That was not going to happen though.

James and I stood there, trying to decide our next move. For most people, that decision would involve two choices, try to cross the rock slide or go back. I would wager that a great majority would choose to go back. For us, the decision involved multiple options for crossing the rock slide, all of which ended with one or both of us, sliding, rolling and tumbling to our death in the river 1,500 feet below.

Enough standing around, I was the first to cross. Before explaining how we crossed the Great Rock Slide of Los Padres, let me try and describe the scene. The hills or mountains of Los Padres are covered in small pine trees, some hardwoods and shrubs. The plant life is not dense and most of the ground is dry and covered in scree (small rocks, sand, and gravel). When the rockslide hit, it began at the top and wiped out almost everything from the top to the river below. In other words, when you looked up from our location, all you saw was a smooth avalanche of rock and gravel, with a few trees standing here and there, which extended all the way to the river. If you had a strong enough piece of cardboard, or a toboggan and enough courage, or stupidity, you could ride that rock slide, accelerating at 32 feet per second until you reached the river and your death below. This is what we were planning on crossing and looking back on it, how stupid we were. But we weren't going back.

I gave James my backpack, took a deep breath, stepped into the rock slide and slid down about five feet. I think I shit myself.

I laid there on that rock slide, sprawled out like a water spider on your pool, my pants soiled. James stood there staring at me wondering if there was anything he could do and what I would do next, besides slide down the hill to certain death. I regained my composure and slowly climbed up the hill so I was once again at the same elevation as the trail and then climbed a few feet higher. The rock slide was about twenty feet across and there was a small tree protruding through the rocks at about the eight-foot mark. Once I climbed up the hill so I was higher than the tree, I began to shimmy across the rock slide towards the tree. Of course, as I shimmied across the slide, I would slide down. After a couple feet, I had to crawl back up the hill. This process went on for about 15 minutes when I finally reached the tree and was able to plant my feet against its trunk and take a break.

James then threw me the backpacks. Obviously, if his throw were bad, or my catch was bad, we would have lost the backpacks and that would have been bad. The alternative though was to try and cross that rock slide with packs on and that was no alternative.

Once the packs were secure in the tree, I climbed up the hill some more and began to shimmy across the last eight feet of the rock slide. I only made it two feet before I was below the trail and had to climb the hill again. Once I was above the trail, I shimmied the remaining distance and stood on hard, level ground. What a great feeling!

I would highly suggest, that whenever possible, you cross, on your belly, a twenty-foot wide rock slide some 1,500 feet.... Wait. On second thought, don't do that; that's stupid.

Once I was secure on the other side, James followed, repeating my process. Upon reaching the tree, he tossed me the packs and then shimmied the final eight feet. During the whole traversing process, James never thought once about his soaked feet. Always a silver lining.

After the rock slide, the trail stayed along the hillside for about a mile until it wound its way down the hills to the river below. Luckily, for James mainly, the trail leveled off about five feet above the river. We then followed the river until we happened upon Last Chance Camp.

Shoes and Socks

What a great campsite! A large, level meadow with a river running alongside; plenty of space and level ground to pitch two tents. There was a large fire ring and of course, plenty of firewood; a benefit of hiking an abandoned trail.

Firewood was certainly a necessity as a roaring fire would be needed to dry James' shoes and socks. Of course, he, had spare socks, but you don't want to pack wet socks. He also packed spare shoes. Not hiking shoes as they would take up a lot of space, but these were "camp shoes", sandals to be worn after a day's hike. He had always brought camp shoes but I didn't see the need. Lighter is better, right? But, with each passing trip, I could see how kicking off your hikers and stretching your toes in sandals made a lot of sense. Not to mention if your hikers ever got soaked, you may need to take them off to dry and then the sandals could provide footwear around the camp. This was my last trip without camp shoes.

After pitching our tents, we gathered the firewood and started the shoe and sock drying fire. James placed his shoes as close to the fire as he dared and hung his socks from sticks standing above the fire. If someone had wandered into our camp, they would have thought socks were on the dinner menu. But of course, we had our Ramen Noodles for dinner and a couple of cups of hot chocolate before calling it a night.

There were no temperatures below freezing that night, no snow or sleet or falling trees. All in all, it was an uneventful night, except for one tick, one small tick that was somewhere a tick should never be. We will leave it at that. After said tick was removed and destroyed, I got a good night's sleep.

The next morning, we awoke, had breakfast, pop-tarts I think, lingered for a while, packed our gear and headed out of Los Padres. Most hikes we leave the way we came, but not Los Padres. We had no desire to shimmy across the rock slide or boulder hop, or wade in James' case, across the river. We took a different trail which took us up the hill and to a road. We then hiked the road back to the parking lot. I don't know if it was an easier hike, but it was dry and a lot less treacherous.

A Commitment Made

Los Padres was our fourth backpacking trip and we had found everything we were looking for; solitude (I think we met two other hikers), scenery, comic relief (James and the River), adventure (crossing the rockslide), a great campsite, and plenty of firewood.

This, of course, didn't mean we were satisfied. Backpacking for us had become an addiction. Once one trip was over, we began discussing the next trip. Where could we go? How far could we push ourselves? Would we freeze? Would we fall into a river? Would we find a rockslide? What would we find? These questions need to be answered and could only be answered in the woods and in the mountains.

With winter waning, we knew we would be backpacking each month, pushing ourselves farther, challenging ourselves. We also knew that all these trips were just a prelude; a prelude to a hike up Mount Whitney.

I can't say exactly when James and I decided to take on Whitney, but at some point, during our weekend in Los Padres, Whitney became our goal. Which is good for me because I like to set goals. That's what I do. I would not say that I'm an achiever and certainly not a great achiever. In fact, I may be considered a cheat as I tend to set goals, I think I can make. All the self-help gurus will tell you to achieve you have to set goals, but the goals need to be something that makes you reach further than you think you may be able. But because you set that goal, which may be just out of reach, you seem to somehow find the extra inches, the extra strength to reach said goal. Of course, for me though, my goals seem to be just within reach and that's how it was for Mount Whitney, or so I thought.

When James and I discussed hiking to the top of Whitney, I thought "That might be tough. Many people have tried and failed. In fact, I think only 20% that attempt makes it to the top. But what the hell, I hike quite a bit, I'm in decent shape, I can make it to the top of Whitney, I'm in". Little did I know that this goal may be out of reach, this goal would make me stretch, physically and mentally, this goal, unlike all those before, would make me change my thinking and make me dig for strength.

But Whitney was months, maybe years, away and it was March and we needed a place to hike.

Girls Trip

Alex, Schmuck 2's daughter, proves that the apple doesn't fall far from the tree

March in Fresno is warm. Daytime temperatures are mostly in the 70's and easily reach the 80's. However, just 40 miles away, and 7000 feet up, it's still winter. Most of Yosemite National Park is still snowed-in and chains are normally required above 5000 feet in Kings Canyon and Sierra National Forests. So, you need to be careful when planning a backpacking trip in March. To avoid the snow, you should stay below 4000 feet and although it may be 75° when you head out, it will certainly get cold during the night. Weather conditions weren't the only thing we needed to consider when planning March's backpacking trip. We were also going to have a couple of new passengers along for the ride.

It seems that James was going home after each of our four previous excursions and wowing his family with tales of awe-inspiring bravery and fortitude. Clearly, he wasn't relaying the truth of our backpacking trips which mostly contained stupidity, arrogance and misfortune. I mean, if our trips were a movie, the movie would be akin to The Great Outdoors or Bill and Ted Go to White Castle. James' tales must have been more akin to The Grey or Vertical Limit. Obviously, James was using his four-hour drive from my house to his house to develop these tales of lore. To be honest, though, this is all conjecture on my part. I have no idea what James did once he got home or what ran through his mind on the way home. But it's the only explanation I can come up with that explains why James' then thirteen-year-old daughter, Alexandra, would want to join us on our backpacking trips. Regardless of her reasons, which probably had more to do with the psyche of a thirteen-year-old girl than her dad's tales, join us she did. So in late March James and I were trying to decide where to backpack, taking into account the weather in the Sierra Nevadas as well as the fact that Alex, and my wife, who had finally thawed from our night in Angeles Forest, would be part of our backpacking troupe.

After some deliberation, it was decided that Panther Creek Trail would be our first "Girls Trip", the name forever synonymous with any backpacking trip that included James daughter and/or my wife, or in other words, any trip that avoided rock slides, foul weather, long distances, strenuous uphill climbs, or anything else that made our backpacking trips worthwhile. As in so many other manly things, our women found a way to sap the machismo from our backpacking trips. But of course, we loved having them along.

Panther Creek Trail is a relatively level, short hike. The trail starts out around 3500 feet and ends at the same elevation, give or take a couple hundred feet. From start to finish the hike is about 3.5 miles. It is actually a very nice day hike, very relaxing with some fantastic views of the Great Divide and some wonderful waterfalls at the end. It's the waterfalls that make it a great backpacking trip. You see, the campsite is in the middle of the waterfalls. No fewer than four waterfalls surround your campsite and there is a raging river of rapids 1500 feet below the campsite. In March, with the snow starting to melt at lower elevations, the falls, and river below are in full flow. The campsite at the end of Panther Creek trail may be the best campsite I have ever had the pleasure to pitch a tent; if not the best, certainly in the top three. There is nothing treacherous about the trail, it is flat and short; a perfect "Girls Trip".

We rolled out of Fresno on Saturday morning with four backpacks, three fully loaded and one partial. To Alex's credit, hers was one of the packs fully loaded, her own sleeping bag of course, but also her own tent. I guess 13-year-old girls don't want to share a tent with dad. I carried the one tent for me and my wife. I was happy to share a tent with Jo because I knew it would be cold at night. After all, Angeles Forest and the 17° night was still in my memory.

We hit the trail around 10 am with the temperature in the mid 60's. The trail starts at the top of a hill and descends, rather steeply to the first of three creek crossings. This first creek is about ankle deep when in full flow. I know its ankle deep because I slipped off what looked like a good stepping point and measured the creek depth with my foot. Of course, those that followed did not use the same stepping point and crossed with no issues. I actually thought Alex would be the first to go in the creek, what with her lineage and James aversion to boulder hopping. Alex's lineage would shine through later in the hike.

After shaking the water from my foot, which would dry quickly due to the warmth of the day, we continued on our hike. This being a Girls Trip, the hike was relatively uneventful. The trail itself is cut into the north side of the North Kaweah Canyon some 1500 feet above the Kaweah River. Most of the trail is exposed to the sun as a majority of the plant life is sagebrush and manzanita.

The second creek in the trail is nothing more than snow run-off and can be crossed easily by stepping on one or two rocks. There were no incidents at the second creek. The third creek on the other hand; that's where the fun is.

The third creek is two to three feet deep, so it's not very treacherous. However, the creek is within 20 feet of a large waterfall. Mentally, you can't help but think that if you go in, you will be swept over the falls.

I was the first to cross and crossed without incident. Why would there be any incident? After all, I've had plenty of practice considering a month earlier we hiked the submerged Los Ponchos trail and I was wearing my non-slip, rock-hugging Montrails. Jo crossed behind me, also without incident. Then came Alex. Knowing Alex was James' daughter, I had my camera poised for the inevitable YouTube moment. Alex's first step was on the rock in front of her and her next step was in the creek to her left. Alex returned to the starting position. Alex's first step was on the rock in front of her and her next step was in the creek to her right. Alex returned to the starting position. On her third try, Alex's second step was on the second rock but her third step was less of a step and more of a stumble back into the creek she had become so familiar with. Alex did not make a fourth attempt at boulder hopping. Alex simply waded across the creek, the waterfall down river be damned. James was beaming with pride.

James then followed his daughter across the creek, nimbly moving from rock to rock, as if to show his daughter that failure is not inevitable.

Within twenty feet of this third creek is the campsite at Panther Creek. The campsite sits atop a small rise a few yards above the aforementioned waterfall. A few yards north of the campsite is a small pool that is fed by three waterfalls, each plunging about 6 feet. The rainbows created in the pool and dancing between the falls are spectacular. The sound of rushing water is all around and is very soothing when it's time to turn in for the night.

We pitched our tents and gathered firewood. Alex found a place in the sun to lay down and dry out. The rest of us explored the area, took cat naps and talked about problems too big for us to solve. As night fell, we continued our conversations around a nice campfire. As the sun went down so did the temperatures, but it never reached "cold", maybe in the Mid-40's.

After a good night's sleep, we hiked out, without incident, the way we came. Our overnight excursion to Panther Creek is the prototypical Girl's Trip.

A couple of years later, my wife, Jaime (a friend and photographer), myself, and our dog Max returned to Panther Creek. Max would not cross the first creek. Max is not a big dog but certainly not a small dog, weighing in about 55 lbs. My wife says he's a Soma dog; he has some of this and some of that. In Max's case, it's a perfect description. He appeared to have part boxer, part shepherd, but pit bull and part whatever else God had left over in his fridge that day. Regardless of his size or lineage, Max was not going to cross that creek. I picked him up and attempted to boulder hop with my 35-pound pack and 55-pound mutt. Max stayed dry. I did not. Due to the embarrassment of being carried across that small creek, Max had no

Max and Schmuck 1 trying to stay dry while crossing creek

problem crossing any other creeks in his path including the one at the head of the falls. Unfortunately, Max contracted cancer a couple years later.

I had to put him down.

To date, it was the hardest day of my life.

I don't think I can ever hike Panther Creek again.

Chilnualna Falls

Alder Wins Again

The falls at Panther Creek is nothing more than a dribble when compared to the raging falls at Chilnualna. Chilnualna Falls is not one long drop like Yosemite or Bridalveil, but a series of drops starting at approximately 8,000 feet and ending at 4,000 feet, at the town of Wawona. Chilnualna Falls is located on the Alder Creek Trail Loop. Yes, THAT Loop. The same loop that was enchanted by witches, had metrological miracles, and broke our spirit. This time, however, we had no plans to complete the loop, no plans to challenge the loop. Our goal was to hike to the top of the falls, spend the night and hike out the way we came. That doesn't mean that somewhere along the way our confidence wouldn't get the best of us and we would once again be thwarted by The Alder Creek Trail Loop.

So, on a clear April Saturday morning, James and I, no girls this time, drove to Yosemite National Park, went to Wawona and headed up the trail. The top of the falls is roughly five miles from the trailhead, 3500 feet up. The trail itself is not very challenging except at the beginning and at the end.

In the beginning, the trail comes face to face with the lower section of the falls. To get around this area, you hike on a rock path made wet and slippery by the mist of the crashing falls. You are not very high, but one wrong step and you will fall into the river below, which is cold, is raging and would certainly cause pain. A child would die falling from that height. To make matters worse, or more exciting to a schmuck, the path is not wide enough to stand with your feet side by side. So, you move along the rock path sideways, attempting to cling to the rock face on your left, which of course is wet, smooth and of no use. You move along this path, slide-stepping, moving slowly, for a few hundred feet and finally break out of the rocks onto a smooth, tree-lined, pine needle covered trail.

For the next few miles, the trail is uneventful, winding its way through the forest, occasionally breaking out to provide great views of the falls. Once near the top, the trail breaks from the woods become rock covered and steep. Here again, you must watch your footing. Although not slippery, you are much higher and the fall would be much more painful. As in the Yosemite Falls trail, the trail here contains steps cut from the rock, which might seem like a good idea, and I'm sure it is, but it can sure mess with your gait and takes a toll on your knees. We slogged through this part of the trail resting often to catch our breath, but even this section was nothing compared to what we endured in the past, or perhaps, we were in better shape after the past five backpacking trips. In either case, we were in our campsite by noon; or we should have been.

Once we arrived at the top of Chilnualna Falls we realized that it was slightly past noon. There was plenty of daylight left for hiking so why stop here? I mean, we had a chance to conquer the loop that beat us badly some seven months earlier. So, we blew through the campsite and headed off to defeat Alder Creek Loop. A witch's cackle filled the woods.

If you recall, this hike took place in April and there is still plenty of snow in the Sierra Nevadas in April and so was the case that day. About half a mile beyond the campsite, and another 500 feet up, we hit the beginnings of snow. Not really bad, some spots here and there. Another half mile and another 500 feet up and the trail was under four feet of the white stuff. Now we were struggling. There was no sign of the trail and no trail markings. We then called upon on our years (more like months) of experience to guide us through the woods hoping that soon the trail would once again reveal itself. We plowed (right word) ahead. The snow got deeper and we got in more trouble. Within two miles of the campsite, we had convinced ourselves that the trail crossed a creek. The creek wasn't visible but we could hear it flowing under the snow. We found a log, snow covered of course, and crossed the unseen creek. How James stayed out of that chilly creek is a mystery, but he did. After a few more yards we found ourselves back at the unseen creek discussing if it made sense to cross again or admit defeat. We tucked our tails between our legs and followed our footsteps back to the safety and warmth of the campsite at the top of Chilnualna Falls. Once again, The Loop defeated us. But that would only add to the glory we felt the day we conquered it.

At the campsite we repeated the routine we have done five times before; collected firewood pitched tents, started a fire, had dinner, talked about problems we could not solve, and then turned in for a fitful night's sleep.

The next morning, we woke to deer in our camp. I don't mean a deer, I mean deer, as in plural, as in many. A deer trail was within 10 feet of our campsite and as we sat there eating breakfast over a crackling fire on a still and crisp morning deer after deer passed through our camp. There were does and buck and even a couple fawns. It was the kind of thing you can only see if you wake with the sun in the middle of the woods. It was the kind of thing that keeps people like us going back into the woods month after month and makes it worth the hardships on the trail.

With the deer still passing through our camp, we packed up our gear and headed back out the way we came. Our spirits were lifted by the deer but a part of us was still burned by our inability to conquer Alder.

You'll Know It When You Hear It

We moved down the trail quickly that morning. The warmth of the sun on our faces, the sight of blue skies and green trees in our eyes, the sound of the crashing falls in our ears; until another sound caught our attention.

I don't know if I can explain what a rattlesnake sounds like, but I can assure you that you'll know it when you hear it. I could not have made that statement earlier in the day, but I am now confident in that statement since we happened upon a rattlesnake sunning itself on the Chilnualna Falls Trail.

James and I were hiking down the falls having a lively discussion about the end of the world and what we would do to resurrect society. It seems must of our on-trail discussions centered on the end of the world and what would be required to bring back humanity. How the world ended would change from time to time; virus, economic collapse, war, etc., but the resurrection of society never changed. Society's resurrection, it's deliverance from the brink, always began with James and me, and anyone lucky enough to seek us out at the end, for those would be the ones to survive. Clearly, our time in the wilderness not only bolstered our belief that we could survive an apocalypse, but it also bolstered the confidence of our loved ones and friends. Crazy is obviously contagious.

So there we were, hiking down the trail talking about building a town and needing to build a fence to keep out the undesirables; the rapists and thieves and those looking to prosper from the end of days. Of course, you can't just keep them out, for that will just fuel their desire to come in. You have to deter them or kill them. But killing people does not seem like a good way to rebuild society. And what of those already in your little hamlet? Surely one or two of those may change over time and wish to have more than is portioned to them. What do you do with the ones inside that decide to steal or commit violence? Do you throw them out thereby sealing their fate but also increasing the numbers of those outside that want inside, or do you kill them, once again starting a society built on death? This is just a sampling of the deep discussions two schmucks have on the trail and the kind of thing that can occupy your mind to the point of almost stepping on a six-foot-long rattlesnake sunning itself on the trail.

But once the rattle went off, all discussion ceased, reality took hold and we were frozen in our steps. It might have been funny if I stopped and James continued, for he would have surely plowed into me, causing me to step forward and within reach of the lunging serpent. But James heard the same hissing and rattling I heard and stopped. We then, without hesitation or discussion, began walking backward. I know I didn't see the snake and I'm sure James did not either, but we did not need to see the impending doom to know we needed to avoid it. After two or three steps back, we both stopped and focused on the rattlesnake in front of us. The snake was uncoiling and began to slither off the trail and into the brush. Now that the snake was retreating, I pulled out my camera, followed the serpent into the brush and took a few photos. Yoda would say, "Stupid is strong in that one".

With the rattlesnake off the trail and documentation of the event secured, we finished the hike down Chilnualna Falls, made it back to the car and headed to the large pizza and vat of Mountain Dew that awaited us in the town of Oakhurst.

A Moment in Time

The Giant Forest

With each successive trip, there would be less and less drama. We stuck to the rules, had the proper footwear and might have been considered "in backpacking shape". After all, when we first started this journey, back at Alder Creek Loop, the best we could hope for was approximately 1 mile an hour, maybe a 1 ½ downhill. Now we were routinely pacing at better than 2 miles an hour up and in some cases hitting 3 on the way down. The loss of drama did not mean the trips were less enjoyable though, it just meant we had more time to enjoy the wonders around us and more time to talk about the impending apocalypse.

One such case was our hike through the Giant Forest in Sequoia National Park. It was memorial weekend and drizzling in Fresno. We knew, since it was drizzling in Fresno, it would be cold in the mountains and perhaps snowing. So, we weren't planning on backpacking that weekend, just a long day hike. Besides, Alex and Jo were with us (another Girl's Trip) so we weren't going to take any chances.

We brought our backpacks, configured for a day hike with only a few essentials and a couple of tents in case we were caught in a storm, and some Gore-Tex® coats to keep us dry. We took 198 into Sequoia National Park. By the time we reached the trailhead, we were immersed in cloud cover. It was dark and damp and cold but we were not miserable. It was too cool to be miserable. I mean the clouds were saturated with water and at lower elevations, it was probably raining. But here in the clouds, the rain wasn't falling, the rain was suspended all around you. Everything had an eerie feeling, but not a scary feeling. You felt like you were walking through some ghost filled forest but not the kind of ghosts that wish to jump out and scare you; more like you might picture on the battlefields of Gettysburg; ghosts still fighting a battle from years past. Of course, our ghosts wouldn't be fighting a battle but might be logging or hunting. Our ghosts would be carrying on their daily chores, ignorant of our existence.

And so, it was as we hiked the five-mile loop of giant trees; ghosts in our minds moving about the forest, the giant trees looking like eerie monoliths marking time, then and now. Occasionally a ray of sun would penetrate the clouds and provide a spotlight, illuminating one warm, bright spot in an otherwise cold, dark world. Each of us would pass through the spotlight soaking up its warmth before the clouds would extinguish its beauty.

From a purely moment in time, scenic standpoint, you can't beat that cold Memorial Weekend in the Giant Forest.

But the Giant Forest wasn't anywhere near our coldest time in the woods. Not even Angeles Forest can claim that title. Our coldest time in the woods was at Jennie's Lake.

Snow in the Lake

Jennie's Lake is not a National Park but it is located within the boundaries of Kings Canyon National Park. Don't know how or why it happened, but a devoted husband named a lake on his property after his wife Jennie and when they created Kings Canyon National Park the lake and land surrounding that lake was allocated to a separate wildlife area and named Jennie's Lake Wildlife Area. It was there that James and I were heading one weekend in June. It was also our first foray into serious elevation in preparation for our trip to Whitney. We were

"Getting High," as our training mantra became on that trip. The importance of acclimating to elevation cannot be overstated when training to hike Whitney. The higher you get, the better your body tolerates the thin air of 14,500 feet of the lower 48's highest summit. And, for us, it started with Jennie's Lake at a shade over 9,000 feet.

The lake is approximately six miles in from the trailhead. There is a strenuous uphill stretch about three miles in but nothing two seasoned backpackers like James and I couldn't handle.

We made good time to the lake and picked a relatively flat spot about 15 yards from the shore to set up camp. The campsite was partially covered in snow and as Jennie's Lake is just over 9,000 feet, snow remains until almost July. We cleared out the snow, set up our tents and collected firewood, then I broke out my surprise: swimming trunks!

Unbeknownst to James, it was my intent for the two of us to take a dip in Jennie's Lake. I knew it would be cold, didn't know how cold, so I thought it would be a once in a moment type thing; take a plunge in a glacial lake (although technically Jennie's Lake isn't glacial, it's close enough). At approximately 1:30 pm on that Saturday in June, James and I were wearing flower covered swim trucks standing on the shore of Jennie's Lake. Schmucks.

We could not walk into the lake as the water temperature was somewhere around 50 degrees and common sense would have driven you back to the shore before you were knee deep. What we needed was to dive in and to do that we needed to find a boulder. Jennie's Lake was happy to oblige by supplying the perfect dive rock, within reach of the shoreline and accessed by two smaller rocks. James went first.

James stepped upon the dive rock in black swim trucks covered with orange flowers. There he stood looking over the lake. I thought he was admiring the view, watching the sunlight shimmer off the clear blue lake when in actuality, he was having serious second thoughts about this endeavor. Second thoughts are in short supply with Two Schmucks on the Trail. Anyway, he noticed that on the other side of the lake, the opposite shoreline was covered in snow and the snow was running off into the lake. It would have been bad enough if the snow-covered shoreline was a pile of snow, but it was a hillside covered in snow. If we had snowboards, we could have ridden off the top of the hill and right into the lake. And all that snow was melting and running into the lake. James retreated to the shoreline.

We laughed for a moment. The kind of laugh that says, "Ha Ha, there is no effing way I'm doing this, ha ha, no way, no how." Being the schmuck he is, second thoughts be damned, James climbed back on the rock.

It's hard to describe his dive into freezing Jennie's Lake. It started out as a normal dive, arms outstretched, hand over hand, fingers pointed. But somewhere in mid-dive, it turned into more of, I don't know, the best description might be a doggy paddle. I mean, James' was horizontal in the air when he decided he did not want to go into the lake. His arms and legs dropped and then his whole body fell, yes fell, into the lake. In an instant, he was standing in the sub 50-degree water and making his way back to shore. James then climbed atop the dive rock and gave me his best muscle man pose. No lie. It's documented.

I thought it was the most hilarious and sad thing I had ever seen, and then I went. I, of course, did not see myself dive but James was kind enough to video the moment and although James' dive was hilarious and sad, mine was worse (or better depending on your perspective). I too, climbed atop the dive rock in my black swim trucks accented in red flowers, and then, like James, tried to turn back in mid-dive and, like James, ended up falling in the lake in perfect doggy paddle position. Not to be outdone, I climbed on the dive rock and gave my best muscle man pose.

Our dives in Jennie's Lake that day, are not something we talk about.

Still freezing from the dives, we made our way to the opposite shoreline, the one covered in snow, found a couple big rocks sticking out of the snow, climbed upon said rocks and bathed in the warmth of the sun.

As we lay in the sun, we discussed our plans to hike to the top of Mount Whitney. We knew to increase our odds of success, we needed to "Get High" and we needed to get over 10,000 feet. That way we could become accustomed to high altitudes and reduce our chances of altitude sickness. To set ourselves up for success, we decided to backpack to the top of Alta Peak.

That night, after warming by the fire, as we lay in our tents, the frogs of Jennie's Lake began to sing us a lullaby which turned into a pop song, and then an anthem and then a cacophony of amphibious rebellion. I have slept outside by many a river and lake but have never experienced the racket that a thousand frogs can make. It was deafening and hysterical.

And just as I was about to climb out of my tent and scream, "Shut Up", a very large mammal, or something, came crashing through the woods. I didn't see said mammal, but I knew what a falling tree sounded like and this didn't sound like that. This was the sound of a large and heavy beast walking across a frozen, snow-covered forest. The sound, this snow crushing, branch breaking sound, started in the distance and then came closer and grew louder and grew so loud that the frogs went silent, and remained silent even as the creature moved away.

We found no tracks in the morning; no evidence of this snow crushing, frog silencing beast. But we now know what a tree falling sounds like, what a rattlesnake sounds like and what a large beast walking across a frozen forest floor might sound like. All three sound like a good reason not to go backpacking, but to us, they are the sounds of adventure.

After searching for evidence of our beast, and finding none, we packed up our gear and headed back the way we came, discussing next month's assault on Alta Peak. Of course, we had that backward.

An Assault

At just over 11,000 feet, Alta Peak was our highest elevation hike to date. Prior to Alta Peak, we never reached 10,000 feet. So, this trip would test our endurance and lung capacity. We were going to get really high.

Alta Peak is located in Kings Canyon National Park and the distance from the trailhead to peak is over six and a half miles. Around four miles in, the trail crosses a stream and it was there that James and I made camp. We didn't know if you could camp on the summit but even if you could, did we really want to carry our full packs all the way to the top. Obviously not.

We set up camp near the stream, unpacked the non-essentials, tent, sleeping bag, sleeping mat, etc., and headed to the top.

For the next mile or so, the trail was relatively level, maybe a slight incline. Then, within a couple miles of the summit, the trail took an abrupt turn upwards. At the time, we didn't know we were within a couple miles of the summit; all James and I knew were that our thighs were burning and our lungs were screaming. But being the manly men we are, we pushed through the pain, which, of course, means we screamed and whined and bitched about the pain, and continued to slog upwards.

It was slow going. We would hike about 20 feet and then rest for 10 seconds; then move forward again and then rest again. We didn't know our elevation, but since there was some plant life, a couple of trees, and some bushes, we surmised that we were still below 10,000 feet which was, to say the least, disheartening.

At a bend in the trail, at the base of a lonely tree (in our minds the 10,000-foot mark) we came upon a young man. He was dizzy, breathing hard and had been throwing up. This was our first encounter with altitude sickness. Luckily, our first encounter was as observers and not participants. The young man assured us that he would be all right and that his friends would soon be back from the summit to help him down the mountain. Don't know if I would use the term friends seeing as they left him at the base of a tree in pain and sickness, but, like his friends, we left him to either get better or perish. He wasn't there when we returned so I assume he survived, or his "friends" pushed his corpse off the edge of the trail; easier than carrying his lifeless body I suppose

After that bend, the lonely tree and sick hiker, it was mainly rock and sand for the next mile or half a mile and that mile, or half a mile, was brutal. The trail had disappeared under gravel and scree.

Very few words match the definition as well as "scree"; a slippery flotsam and jetsam mashup of rock fragments, gravel, dust, dirt, and sand that has accumulated due to erosion and rock slides. Besides reducing its definition to one perfect word, mouthing the word "scree" also gives one the perfect indication of the pain one feels while trying to cross a rock fragment, gravel, dust and dirt field. Each step introduced more scree into our shoes. Every slip of the feet, mainly caused by the aforementioned scree in our shoes, would force us to regain our balance by placing our hands in the scree field, thereby injecting rock fragments into our hands. There was, and is, nothing pleasant about crossing the field of scree.

We could see the summit so we knew which way to go, we just could not get there. If we tried to go straight up, which of course we did, we would sink in the gravel and slowly slide down. If we tried to go left or right and slowly move up the mountain, the gravel would give way and we would slowly slide down. It did not matter our course, we were going to move up slowly and move down slowly. We were not assaulting Alta Peak; Alta Peak was assaulting us. We had to keep pushing ourselves forward. Take a couple steps and dig our feet in or else we may give up any real estate achieved. We kept pushing onward, our backs bent over so we were leaning into the mountain, our feet more sideways than forward so we had maximum resistance against the sliding gravel. Up we went, three steps forward, stop to rest, slide two feet, three steps forward, stop to rest, slide two feet; you get the picture.

But we would not be deterred. We could see people sitting on the summit. We could gauge the distance. We understand the struggle necessary to achieve the goal. And after an hour or two of beginning our assault through the gravel and scree, we had reached the summit of Alta Peak. We had broken the 10,000-foot barrier and we were not suffering from altitude sickness.

Goal achieved. Limits pushed. Confidence raised.

No matter where you go, someone is always watching

Although it took a great effort for us to conquer Alta Peak, all in all, our backpacking trips were easier. We were hiking seven or eight miles by noon, making camp, taking naps, hanging out and then returning the next morning. We had swum in freezing lakes, broke the 10,000-foot barrier, challenged ghosts in the woods, traversed raging rivers (or lazy streams). We needed more. We wanted more. But unfortunately, life sometimes interrupts our great plans and because of life, James and I would not get back into the woods until winter.

It's Still All About the Shoes

Valley Floor

By the time James and I dealt with our life issues, it was November and most trails were snowed in or the trail heads were inaccessible. We had driven south and west the past winter, but didn't want to lose that kind of hiking time on the road. The Yosemite Valley floor is risky in November, but worth a shot, so we took it.

The valley floor sits at 4500 feet but is still accessible in the early winter. The roads are open to the valley, although you may need chains. On this particular Saturday in November, chains were not necessary, neither were snowshoes.

We drove to the Bridalveil Falls parking lot and proceeded to hike the six-mile Valley Floor Loop. The valley floor is relatively level and the loop will take you past Bridalveil Falls, Cathedral Rock, The Three Brothers, El Capitan, and the Merced River. It is the perfect day hike and the trail is empty during November.

El Capitan shrouded in clouds

Our packs carried essentials and emergency gear; food, tent, space blanket. It was easy going and the silence and scenery were surreal. As we sat along the Merced River, not quite frozen over, clouds were hanging on El Capitan. Sunlight was pushing through the clouds, lighting the mammoth face and dancing on the river. Everywhere was silence. Majestic rock formations on your left and right framed the valley like giant soldiers protecting the village below.

Nothing interrupted the perfection that day.

Big Baldy

In January, the road to Yosemite Valley was closed, so we headed to Kings Canyon National Park. The road into Kings Canyon was open but unless you were planning to go to Grant's Grove, an awesome loop of Sequoias, you would need chains. Although Grant's Grove is awesome, it is paved, packed with tourists and short. We wanted solitude and we wanted to try snowshoes.

Neither James nor I have ever snowshoed. Since neither of us has backpacked and we were now doing that, we thought we would try snowshoeing. So, we each rented a pair of snowshoes, packed our packs with essential and emergency items and headed to Kings Canyon. We didn't have a trail or location in mind. We thought, since everything's covered in snow, there are no real trails, so we would park the truck and hike into the woods.

We drove into Kings Canyon, made a right onto Grant's Road, ignored the sign that read "Tire Chains Required" (after all, ignoring warnings worked so well for us in the past) and drove until we came upon a trail sign that read "Big Baldy". The distance to Big Baldy was about two and a half miles from the trailhead so it would be a perfect trail for snowshoe novices like us. We parked the truck on the side of the road (bad idea when a U-turn is required), strapped on our snowshoes (should have listened to clerk during his spiel about putting on snowshoes), threw on our day packs and headed into the woods.

The hike was a relatively easy once you learned how to walk in snowshoes. Mine were on upside down. Once corrected I stayed on top of the snow and made better time.

I can't say for sure if we ever were on top of Big Baldy. There was no sign and the snow was roughly seven feet deep, so there were no granite or rock outcroppings. But from our location, everything around us went straight down. We could go no further and I believe we were on top of the aforementioned rock.

Above the clouds on Big Baldy

The amazing thing about that day was the cloud cover. Big Baldy is at roughly 8,200 feet and the clouds were at 8,120 feet and they were thick and dark. In fact, we were standing in sunshine under clear blue skies and below us, it was snowing or raining, depending on your elevation. The clouds were so thick that you could not see through them. When you looked out or down from Big Baldy, all you saw were gray, puffy clouds and they weren't moving. It appeared as if we were standing on the clouds. The only way one could tell we weren't on the clouds, was because you could see the rise of Big Baldy and therefore knew we were above the clouds.

After documenting this moment, we sat down for lunch. We both had tripod stools. James' stool supported him above the snow and kept his ass dry. My stool sunk in the snow immediately. My ass was not dry. You see, his stool has a piece of cloth at the bottom of the three legs attached to each leg, forming a web. My stool had no such cloth. James' stool supported him above the snow. My stool was used to measure the depth of the snow, which was ass deep that day. My new stool now has a web. Its little learning moments like this that separates the Schmucks from the real pros.

After lunch, we hiked out to my truck. We loaded up and I proceeded to make a U-turn so we could leave the way we came. The trailhead for Big Baldy is on a curve, and a banked curve at that. I ignored the "Chains Required" sign. So, when I made the required U-turn, I got perpendicular to the road, slid down the road and nosed into the roadside snow bank. No problem, I placed the truck in reverse, backed up about three feet and slid nose first back into the roadside snow bank. No problem, I placed the truck in reverse, backed up about three feet and slid nose first into the roadside snow bank. I repeated the aforementioned process about three times, cussing sufficiently enough after each plunge into the snow bank to ensure God knew just how I felt about snow, snow chains, and everything frozen.

James got out of the truck to see what he could do and watched me repeat the process three more times. Apparently, he just wanted to watch the show of me sliding into the snow bank again and again and yet again all the while enjoying my head-bobbing cursing and arm flailing frustration in the cab as the truck plowed into the road side snow bank repeatedly due to a lack of traction. He's outside laughing like a drunken monkey while I am in the cab cursing gravity and the ice-covered road. Nice.

By now I had admitted defeat and was going to use the chains. Of course, I had chains, but they were borrowed from my neighbor and they fit a Humvee. I have a four-cylinder Isuzu; basically, a toy truck when compared to a Humvee. I only brought the chains in-case a ranger checked, I did not plan to actually use them but it was good that I brought them, not because I was stuck and nosed into a snow bank. No, it was good that I had them because about the last time I slid into the bank, Ranger Jane came around the corner.

Of course, it was Ranger Jane. What else could explain my current predicament? Ranger Jane pulled over to ask what we were doing but she actually wanted to see if her spell had sufficiently destroyed our desire to enter her woods. The situation needed no explaining, so we simply told Ranger Jane we were installing tire chains so I could get my truck headed in the right direction. This of course was a lie since the chains I had were made for a behemoth of a truck and I was driving a bird of a truck. Ranger Jane watched us as I laid the chains in the snow behind my rear tires and backed onto the chains and then over them, giving me enough distance from the snow bank to turn my truck parallel with the road. I then threw the chains in the back of the truck, told Ranger Jane we were leaving and thanked her for her help; all very sarcastically of course. Man, I hate witches.

Once we finally got going in the right direction, we kept it slow and constant and were able to leave the snow behind for dry pavement.

We headed down 180 out of Kings Canyon. During the drive to Bear Pizza in Squaw Valley, we decided we needed, not wanted but needed, to push ourselves and our new-found love affair with snowshoes and to do that, we needed a mountain. And because Whitney was the goal, we need to get high.

Go On Without Me

"Go on without me!" That's what he said. James had reached his limit. He hit the wall. His endurance was no more. No more muscles. No more drive. No more intestinal fortitude. I was to leave James at the base of the tree as I scaled the few remaining yards to the top of Mount San Jacinto.

Mount San Jacinto is located in Palm Springs, California; Southern California; in the desert. Not really a place known for its snow, but snow it has; on the top of Mount San Jacinto. San Jacinto is at almost 11,000 feet but you don't have to hike the entire distance. A tram will take you from the desert floor to a ski lodge at about 8,500 feet. You have to hike the remaining 2,500 feet up, and we did, almost, in snowshoes.

After getting off the tram and letting James regain his color and composure, as James is not fond of heights, we dodged the crowd of would-be skiers and snow revelers and headed off to find a trail that would lead us to the San Jacinto summit. Snowshoes weren't required in the first mile or so of the hike, as the snow was well compacted, after that, however, snowshoes were a must, better yet, a snowplow would have been ideal.

We clipped on our snowshoes, took about fifteen steps and realized we had no idea where we were going. There was no trail, just snow. No one had gone before us to show us the way. There was only snow. Six feet high. Everywhere you looked, and as far as you could see, there was snow. If we were going to the top, if anyone was going to the top, someone, or more specifically two schmucks, would have to cut the trial. And by cut, I mean use your feet and legs to push, dig, plow the snow from in front of you as you make the multi-mile trek to the top.

But of course, we had snowshoes. We would walk on top of the snow and not sink three and four feet into the snow. Which would have been correct if we rented the available "wings" for the snowshoes thereby increasing the surface area of the shoe. But of course, being the schmucks that we are, we did not rent the wings, did not increase the surface area of the snowshoes, and; thereby, did not walk on top of the snow. We had to push, dig and plow our way to the top. It took us no less than five hours to reach what we thought was the summit that day.

One of us would cut the trail until we no longer could move our legs. With each step, we would sink three to four feet. We would lift our sunken snowshoes out of snow-holes we created just to have them sink another three or four feet through the powder. After a few steps, we would be so tired that we could not fully lift our snowshoes out of the snow-holes and our snowshoes would catch the top portion of the snow and we would face-plant. This, of course, would result in a benefit of not having to cut the next five feet of trail as well as provide a refreshing relief to the sweat pouring from our faces. The person following the leader would not have as difficult a time as they would step in the leader's tracks. Once the leader was too tired, signified by the face-planting exercise, the follower would then take the lead and the leader would follow. This game of snowshoe leap-frog continued as we went up and up and up the mountain.

As if the game of snowshoe leap-frog isn't exhausting enough, we had the benefit of a 2,500-foot of elevation gain. There were times that the hike was too steep and James and I would have to create our own switchbacks in order to move up the mountain. There were times the hike was so draining that we would just stop and wonder aloud if we would, could, make it the top. Those pauses made the hike worthwhile.

When we would stop, we could see the beauty and majesty of Mount San Jacinto. When we were moving, our faces were down watching every stop, either trying to ensure that we lifted our feet high enough to clear the snow bank in front of us or either ensuring that each step landed in the snow depression left by the person in front. But when we stopped and raised our heads, the stillness was beautiful. Everything was covered in virgin, white snow. There were no clouds in the sky, no fog. Crayola Crayons developed the color Sky Blue based on the color of the sky that day. It wasn't "cold", but you could feel the air on your face. It made you feel young like you could pass any challenge, you could persevere, you could hike in snowshoes to the top of Mount San Jacinto. Of course, my face wasn't the body part hiking and my thighs could give a damn what the air felt like. So, before the thighs would stiffen, we would take our eyes from the beauty around us, direct them to the three feet in front of our feet, and start plowing ahead.

Up we went. Sometimes straight-up, sometimes zig-zagging our way up, but all the time up. Then we could go up no further. There was no more up, only down the other side. We were standing on a ridge admiring the view and congratulating each other for pushing our way to the top. A few moments later, some lackeys that didn't have to cut in the trail made it to our position, thanked us for cutting in the trail and then asked us if we were going to the top.

"Going to the top? We're at the top."

"Sorry, the top is that way about 200 yards. See you there."

Son...of a bitch.

James and I looked at each other, hoping one would say let's go home, realized that we couldn't come this close just to fail, and turned to hike to the top. Luckily, the last 200 yards should be relatively simple as the lackeys were now cutting in the final trail. Of course, relative is relative and after spending minutes on what we thought was the top, our thighs tightened, our vigor vanished and our drive disappeared. James went down.

Schmuck down! Schmuck down!

This was not a face plant. This was, "I give up-I'm not going any further-go on without me," plant. I was laughing, once again at James' expense, because I thought he was kidding, but he was not going to get-up, he was not going to hike the remaining yards. James was done.

I often think back to that moment and think that I should have listened to James and left him there, hiked to the top, stood on the summit, returned and hiked out with him. After all, our goal was to reach the summit and we did not, so we failed. But it didn't, and doesn't, feel like a failure. That day was spectacular. The scenery was tranquil and beautiful. The camaraderie was a brotherhood. How can that kind of day be a failure? It was the kind of day you're always looking for but rarely, if ever, find. I would snowshoe within 200 yards of the Mount San Jacinto summit every day, and twice on Sunday, if each time, the day was like that Saturday in February.

James and I sat there, with the summit, our goal, in clear view, had some lunch and headed down the mountain. As you can imagine, the trip down was much faster than the trip up. Not only was the trail abundantly clear, but it was also extremely steep. Each time you picked up one snowshoe, you would slide down about two feet before planting your step. When we came to areas that we zig-zagged, we went straight down. We made great time going down the mountain and were able to stop for a little dinner down in the lodge. There's nothing like a $10 burger and an $8 beer after snowshoeing up and down a mountain.

Once at the bottom, and James regained his natural color and balance, we discussed our next hike, which we knew would be snowless. We knew our next hike would be a backpacking trip. It was time to test those limits we were so proud of; those limits we exalted after conquering Alta Peak. We needed to test ourselves and that test came in the form of Hell For Sure Pass, a hike that would take us three days and severely test James' aversion to horses.

An interesting Post-Script to the story of Mount San Jacinto: I later learned that James was experiencing severe chest pains at several points throughout the hike and they became more acute as we ascended. Of course, he said nothing about it at the time so as not to ruin the trip; but, apparently, these chest pains freaked him out to the point that he immediately booked a visit to a cardiologist. After a stress test and a battery of other examinations, nothing serious was found and he was given the green light for a bid on Whitney.

Let's Ramp It Up
Sleepy Hollow

Hell for Sure Pass is the name given to the crevice of rocks, boulders and stream you must assail in Kings Canyon National Park from the Dickey Creek Wilderness. From the trailhead to the pass is approximately 15 miles and we found ourselves on that trailhead on July 4th weekend.

The hike begins by crossing the Dickey Creek Dam, an easy enough crossing unless your uncomfortable with heights, which of course James is, but once on the other side he was good, albeit a little green. After crossing the dam, the trail wanders through scenic flat land and then enters the forest. There is a stream at the entrance of the forest and boulders are well placed so you can stay dry. Due to James' aversion to boulder hopping, James did not stay dry as he chose (as if he had any other choice) to wade through the water.

Once in the woods, the trail rises slightly. The incline is noticeable but not strenuous. What is noticeable, however, are all the hoof prints. Hoofprints created by horses. Obviously, the trail to Hell for Sure Pass is a favorite of horseback riders and pack animals. This was no issue for me but as I was learning, James is not a fan of horses. I don't know why he has such an intense dislike of horses. I don't know if it's the damage they do to trails, the piles of shit they leave behind or some traumatic event that occurred between a horse and a much younger James. In any case, he was not happy when we chanced upon our first majestic steed coming down the trail.

The horse looked like any horse you've seen; about 5 ½ feet tall at the shoulders, chestnut brown, big eyes, long tail. There were no fangs, no claws, no fire coming from its nostrils. The rider was a cowboy; jeans, Stetson, flannel shirt. All in all, the horse and rider were very generic. In James' eyes though, he must have been looking at Ichabod Cranes' nemesis; a 9-foot-tall, black steed with fire for eyes supporting a headless, caped rider. I say this because as soon as the horse came into sight, James dropped his eyes and moved off the trail. I don't mean, took a step of the trail, I mean moved off the trail and continued to move off until he was 15 feet into the woods and still retreating. After the horse and rider passed, James made his way back to the trail, raised his eyes and said, "I don't like horses". I felt sorry for James because we would encounter no fewer than three more horses that day and there were still two days left in the hike.

With James' nightmare fading behind us, we pushed on to Hell for Sure Pass; more exactly, Rainbow Lake. As mentioned earlier, the Pass is fifteen miles from the trailhead and although we were in much better shape these days and could have made the pass in one day, it was not our desire to do so. We wanted to spend some time in the wilderness, take a leisurely hike. So, our plan was to make camp at Rainbow Lake, about 10 miles in. We would then hike to Hell for Sure Pass the next day and hump it out the third day.

Besides the occasional horse, to the subsequent annoyance of my hiking partner, our hike to Rainbow Lake was uneventful. In all honesty, though, I can't be sure that we camped at Rainbow Lake. There are three lakes in the same vicinity: Rainbow, Rainer, and Thompson. The guidebook, like most, or all, guidebooks was not very clear as to the sequence of the lakes; hence my uncertainty. But we stopped at the first lake we came upon and set up camp.

We arrived somewhere near four in the afternoon. Not as soon as we could have made it, what with James' retreating into the woods every time a horse came down the trail. But we made decent enough time and were rested enough to gather firewood and pitch our tents. That evening was very relaxing. The frogs provided a spontaneous symphony and the conversation between James and I was, as always, lively and centered on the end of the World (can you have a lively conversation about death?). By now, I knew that we were secretly hoping for the end of the World. Those close to us knew it was no secret.

The next morning, we decided on a new course of action. If we learned anything during our trips into the wilderness, spontaneity, and adaptability are key when backpacking. Not so coincidently, the same two indispensable traits are required during the apocalypse.

We decided to leave camp and hike to the top of Hell for Sure Pass, then return and spend the night at the same location, hiking out the next day.

So, with a few essentials thrown in our backpack, mainly food and water, we went to "Get High.".

The Pass is at over 11,000 feet and overlooks the Red Lake Basin. As you hike through the basin, you pass shimmering blue lakes, surrounded by the greenest grasses and an explosion of orange wildflowers. As you gain elevation, the grasses give way to rock and the wildflowers give way to orange and yellow lichen, but the lakes are still crystal clear and clean enough to drink. It is a gorgeous area, especially when viewed from the top of the Pass.

But like anything worthwhile, you will have to work for that view.

Difference Between Light and Dark

From the Red Lake Basin, the trail goes up. Not gradually up, not rising up, not even switch-back up. Think of a fireman's ladder up. That is how steep the climb is to the top of the Pass. The trail goes up through a creek that is flowing down between the crevice formed by the meeting of two mountains. Of course, when these mountains collided or rose together, some 10,000 years ago, many a boulder and rock were jarred free and now sit within this crevice. You cannot see the trail, you can only sense the trail once you're in the creek. If the water is flowing down over your shoes, then you are on the trail. If you have to step around rocks and climb over boulders, then you're on the trail. If after twenty feet into the ascent, you're asking each other if all this work will be worth it, you're on the trail. And once we reached the top, all the work and ten times more was worth the view.

As mentioned earlier, Hell for Sure Pass is the pass between Dickey Creek Wilderness and Kings Canyon National Park. At the top of the pass, you can literally straddle the Wilderness and the Park. On the one side, you have the Red Lake Basin; blue lakes, green grasses, orange, and yellow plant life. On the other side, you have the moon; grays and blacks, no life, only desolation. I can't say that it's two sides of the same coin even though it's two sides of the same mountain. After all, both sides of a coin have design and signs of life. One side of the coin, a person and the other side, an eagle or building built by a person. The Kings Canyon side of the mountain had no life. I can't even say it had death because death implies that there was life at one time. There was never any life on the Kings Canyon side of Hell for Sure. A moon landscape is a perfect description. The only semblance of humankind on the moon landscape of Kings Canyon is the trail winding its way down the mountain to what surely must be forested areas. I cannot imagine the effort it would take to climb that landscape. The gravel and scree that covered that side of the mountain made our time at Alta Peak look like child's play. If Mount Whitney's landscape was anything like what I was viewing at the top of Hell for Sure Pass, then I needed a new goal.

I can't explain why the landscapes were completely different. I assume it's because the prevailing winds cause the clouds to drop all their moisture on the west side of Hell for Sure leaving nothing for the east side. Regardless of the reason, it was the perfect metaphor for the end of time as there was life on one side, today's world, and the absence of life on the other side, the world after the apocalypse. We had lunch on the top of the pass and continued planning our new society.

After lunch, we scampered down and made our way back to our lake side camp site. It was still relatively early, sometime around three, so we decided to break camp and make our way down the trail thereby reducing the distance needed to hike out the next day.

Like the hike in to "Whatever" Lake, the hike back was uneventful; except for the two or three times James scampered into the woods trying to avoid horses and the fact that my pack had become a torture device.

When you purchase your first pack, any well-intentioned guidebook, internet article, or pack salesperson will tell you that, "The pack should ride on your hips". After all these years I still don't know exactly what that means but I can tell you that on our hike back from "Whatever" Lake, the pack was not on my hips. In fact, I don't think the pack was in the vicinity of being on my hips. The pack was hanging from my shoulders, pulling on my back, tugging on my neck and digging into my sides. I did not have a pack on my back. I had a live animal, a bear cub, hanging around my neck.

Knowing that we were "moving" camp, I did not take the time to pack my pack correctly. I did not put my sleeping bag at the bottom, my tent on top of my sleeping bag, my spare clothes and pillow on top of that, my food items and cook items and miscellaneous items on top of that. I just threw everything into my pack and stuffed in my tent and sleeping bag and suffered for the next 6 miles. And, being one of two schmucks on the trail, I did not stop during those 6 miles and repack. Although not a law, or truism, or maxim, it is very important to take the time, every time, to pack your pack correctly and make sure it's riding on your hips. I may not be able to describe what "riding on your hips" means, but you will know when it's not "on your hips".

Upon reaching the stream at the edge of the woods I was tired of wrestling with the bear on my back so we decided to make camp. There was a well-used camp area near the creek. A well-used *horse* camp. Because it was so well used there was a shortage of firewood in the immediate vicinity. There was not, however, a shortage of horse shit. Trying to set-up tents that did not rest upon horse shit was like trying to fall out of a boat without hitting the water. I'm exaggerating a little because, after some effort, we were able to clear an area of enough shit so we could set-up our tents. Unfortunately, though, we could not clear the area of horse shit smell. Needless to say, it was not one of our favorite campsites, especially considering the fact that two horses entered the camp area during the evening and added to the horse shit stench. Now I understand why James does not like horses.

The next morning, we awoke, not well rested and not feeling like lingering over coffee and horse shit. We quickly packed up, correctly this time, and headed out of the woods, across the meadow, over the damn, back to the car and down to our favorite pizza joint in Squaw Valley.

The beauty of the basin as you look over your shoulder while ascending Hell-For-Sure-Pass

With the conquest of the 11,000-foot Hell for Sure Pass, and the previous assault on Alta Peak, our confidence was high, our bravado was strong. Normally this would spell certain doom, but we were different. We were still two schmucks, but we were two schmucks that, through disaster and many mistakes, finally understood the strengths, fortitude, constitution and equipment needed to backpack. We were ready to prove our skills on the one trail that had beaten us twice. We were ready to conquer our nemesis. We were Superman and we were going to beat Lex Luthor: The Alder Creek Trail Loop.

We Will Dominate

The Best Lunch Spot in the Country

Alas, Lex Luthor would have to wait though. The girls, Jo and Alex, wanted to go on another excursion. So, we decided to revisit North Dome.

There is more than one way to the top of North Dome. Earlier, an October two years ago, James and I took the most difficult route, up Yosemite Falls; definitely not a Girl's Trip. This time, with Jo and Alex along, we chose to take a more direct route, south, downhill from Tioga Road; definitely a Girl's Trip.

As mentioned earlier in this accounting, Tioga Road is not a pleasant road for those with an inclination towards motion sickness and when I say those, I mean James. In fact, there are no good roads in Yosemite National Park when up and down, and left and right, and up and down, and left and right, leads one to nausea and the violent symptoms that may follow. But he understood, and understands, that without pain there can be no gain; so, James sucks it up and takes some Dramamine every time we head into Yosemite and today would be no different.

With James well medicated, we headed into Yosemite, down Wawona Road, pass Yosemite Valley, and turned East, on to Tioga Road. A few miles East on Tioga Road, an eternity for anyone with motion sickness, we found ourselves at the North Dome trailhead.

From the trailhead to the top of North Dome is four to five miles and except for the thirty yards up North Dome, it is all downhill. Ok, not all downhill but it *trends* downhill. We hit the trail at eight on a Saturday morning in August determined to have lunch in the sunlight atop North Dome, and so we did.

We all made good time, a sure sign that the girls were also in backpacking shape. There were no incidents on the trail and only one detour.

Yosemite National Park has two natural rock arches. One is underwater and the second is located about a mile off the North Dome from Tioga Road trail. We took the side trip, dropped our packs at the bottom of a hill and made the strenuous climb to the natural rock formation. All of us climbed on top of the arch, except for our resident acrophobic, documented the moment and retreated to the base of the hill to retrieve

Schmuck 1 on top of the arch. Schmuck 2 on the side of the arch.

our backpacks and continue on to North Dome.

I realize that these accountings of our backpacking exploits may indicate that James is a city-fied nerd and not suited for outdoor adventure; what with his inability to boulder hop, his dislike of horses, his aversion to heights, and his chronic motion sickness. But I can assure you that what James may lack in constitutional durability he more than makes up for in comedy relief, insight into human nature, intelligence regarding organizational politics, and his inexplicable desire to endure backpacking in the wilderness with a schmuck like me. Believe me, You want James on your team when the World goes to shit. He's also funny and some would say good-looking. I wouldn't, but some would.

With our packs on our backs, we completed the hike to the base of North Dome and made camp where James and I made camp roughly two years earlier. We then scampered to the top of North Dome and had lunch. Once again, the view from the top of North Dome was absolutely breathtaking; the sun was dancing off the Merced River in the valley below and casting hues of yellow, gold and silver on the sheer face of Half Dome across the valley. The valley entrance was guarded by the Three Brothers and El Capitan. I don't think there's a better place to have lunch in all the World.

Jo sitting on North Dome-Half Dome in background

We spent the remaining daylight hours collecting firewood and taking short hikes around the dome. As night fell, we started the fire and again talked about big problems we couldn't solve. We stayed away from conversations involving viruses, economic collapse and war as a 13-year-old was in our group; not that Alex couldn't handle the conversation, but girls in high school should not be worried about such adult things around a perfect campfire and a perfectly still night. After a good night's sleep, we packed up and headed out to Tioga Road. Although we did not stop to climb the arch, it took a little longer to get out than get in because we were going up-hill. But the elevation is not very great so there was no drama. James popped a couple Dramamine and although our bodies were headed to Oakhurst for pizza and Mountain Dew, James' and my mind were headed to The Alder Creek Trail Loop.

Superman vs Lex Luthor

When James and I awoke that Saturday morning in October, we had one thing on our collective mind – we were not going to lose to the Alder Creek Trail Loop. We lost twenty-four months ago and The Loop beat us again nineteen months ago, but this weekend was going to be different. And although we knew we were going to beat the loop, we had no idea that we were going to destroy the Alder Creek Trail Loop.

This time, we had a plan. It was a good plan. We did not stick to the plan. We're schmucks! What did you expect? But we did have a plan. On Saturday we would hike to the high point of the trail, three miles past Deer Creek camp, the site of our first failure, make camp in Turner Meadow, and then on Sunday, hike the three miles to Chilnualna Falls, the site of our second failure, and then hike downhill and complete the Alder Creek Trail Loop.

We hit the trailhead at nine in the morning and all went as planned. We did not struggle as the trail rose before us. With full packs and full hearts; we dominated. We talked and laughed and posed for pictures as we made our way to the high point of the trail. There were no incantations from Ranger Jane or her coven. They didn't know we were there as we no longer registered before we hit the trail and we no longer carried useless bear canisters. Therefore, we weren't battling meteorological demons, mud, and raging rivers. It was just two men, strong and determined, facing a somewhat subdued Mother Nature.

We hit Turner Meadow at noon. Then we did what all good schmucks do: we changed the plan. We stood in the trail at Turner Meadow, enjoying the peace and silence. I turned to James and said: "You know; we could make Chilnualna by nightfall."

"Really?" He replied, incredulous.

"Yep. It's all downhill from here. We could do it."

"Hell," he said. "I'm in!"

We decided that we would hike to Chilnualna Falls and make camp there unless we reached the head of the falls before nightfall. If that were the case, we would hike out that day!

With lunch in our stomach and a new plan in our minds, we pushed on. We were Butch and Sundance ready to take on the Bolivian Army. Of course, things didn't end so well for those two schmucks Butch and Sundance, so there's that.

We were cruising through the woods, making great time. We had hit the Loop's high point so now the trail was either level or descending. We were eclipsing three miles an hour. Then the Bolivian Army arrived. Not literally of course, but figuratively in the form of a black bear.

I was the first to see it. James noticed the beast after he walked into me and asked why I had stopped. The black bear was no more than thirty yards in front of us and was right on the trail; not to the left or right, not downhill or uphill, but right in the middle of the trail. I have no idea if the bear was big or small for a black bear. Don't know if he/she was an adult. But it was a bear and it was stopping us from completing the Alder Creek Trail Loop. Somewhere Ranger Jane was cackling.

The bear had no idea of our presence as it was shredding a log and eating the insects within. Why a beast with claws strong enough, long enough and sharp enough to rip apart wood as well as a man's throat, would want to eat termites is beyond me. Then again, I'm not a bear. Besides being oblivious to our presence, it was also oblivious to time and certainly completely oblivious to our well-laid plans. I believe, as George Carlin did, that animals have no concept of time. To them, everything is forever; which is why dogs are so happy when you come home. When you left, your dog thought you would be gone forever and when you returned, you were home forever; hence the wagging tail and wiggling body. Since the bear before us was planning to eat forever, time meant nothing to it. James and I, on the other hand, knew all about time. After all, we had watches that told us what time it was on the trail.

Hell, we could tell you the time in Bolivia. As it happened, the bear decided to have a snack in the trail right around 4:00 pm, local. The sun would set around 5:30. We had no clue how much time we needed to get to Chilnualna Falls. But we knew we couldn't get to the falls with a black bear on the trail.

So, there we stood. Watching a black bear feed. Hoping he/she would eat enough and not need see us as a protein supplement. We stood there, watching the sun go down; watching The Alder Creek Loop beat us again. We weren't only watching though. We were planning. Planning how to move the bear; how to intimidate the bear. We could grab some sticks and make a racket swinging around wildly. We could approach the bear screaming and shouting and "looking big". We had to do something as we were not going to fail. Then, without notice, and without warning, the bear, the demon sent to thwart us, picked up his/her head, stared at James and I and ran off into the woods! Clearly, our determination, our bravado, our willingness to take on the great beast showed like some great, bright aura around us and scared the great beast back from whence it came. Ranger Jane had been melted.

With more confidence than we had a right to, we pushed onto the head of Chilnualna Falls making the falls an hour later. We had just about 30 minutes before darkness would envelop the lands. Could we make the five-mile hike down in thirty minutes? Would the moon supply enough light to guide us to safety? Would Ranger Jane reappear or send one of her demons to destroy us in the darkness of the woods? Who cares? We were going to be victorious and we headed down the trail and into the woods as the sun set and darkness overtook us.

There are many forms of darkness; many hues and depths. There is the darkness we experience when all the lights are off and slivers of sunlight pass through covered windows. It is not bright, but there is enough light to navigate. There is also the darkness we experience when you wake up in the middle of the night. At first, you see nothing, but then your eyes open wider to let in light from the stars, or the moon peering through the window, or to let in the light being given from your alarm clock or night lite. You certainly can't read or write by that light, but you can make your way to the bathroom or the kitchen for a bite to eat. Then there is the darkness of a tomb. The blackness of the grave. No light enters. You see nothing. That is the hue of darkness we experienced when the sun went down and we were still on the Alder Creek Loop Trail. There was no moon that night. There were no stars that night. Only darkness and two hikers trapped in that darkness. Ranger Jane may have melted, but her coven was using all their remaining powers to keep us from completing the loop. We wondered if that bear was following us.

But we had learned our lessons and we were prepared. James had a headlamp and I had a generator flashlight. James' headlamp would provide us with about four feet of light and my flashlight, when fully wound, would provide about six feet of light. James took the lead and we lit the trail best we could. We did not move the light into the surrounding woods for fear of seeing the eyes that were watching us. James' headlamp dimmed halfway down the falls so I moved to the front and kept cranking my flashlight. We moved slowly, avoiding roots and rocks and all items cast before us by the followers of Ranger Jane.

Soon we came upon a fork in the trail. To the left was the lower section of the falls and the rock path that would surely cause us to fall to our death. To the right was a pack trail that was paved and would help us avoid the aforementioned peril. After a brief discussion, we decided we were going to beat our nemesis; there was no reason to embarrass it. So we turned right and followed the pack trail to the town of Wawona and the trails end.

We had done it! We had succeeded where we had failed twice before. We not only completed the Alder Creek Trail Loop with full backpacks, we completed the loop in eleven hours. We were the Magnificent Seven and we destroyed the Mexican Army and lived to tell the tale. We were Superman and not only defeated Lex Luger, we killed the SOB. James and I stood in the town of Wawona, in the darkness and raised our arms in victory. We danced like Cassius Clay. We moved like Rocky Balboa. We flipped-off the trail and the witches sworn to protect it. The people of Wawona called the police. We high-tailed it to the truck.

We dominated the Loop and we were ready for Mount Whitney.

Hiking in Anticipation

Cut This….

We were pumped. We were psyched. We were ready to take on Mount Whitney. But Whitney would have to wait. It was October and there is snow on Whitney in October. Also, you need a permit to hike Mount Whitney and the permits are dispersed using a lottery system which only accepts applications in February. We decided to take on the legendary mountain in August. So, we had ten more months to prepare for Whitney; ten more backpacking trips to test our skills. We only needed two.

Since it was winter and since we enjoyed our previous snowshoeing hikes, we decided to spend a day in January hiking to Dewey Point from Glacier Point Road, in Yosemite National Park.

Many people, during all four seasons, make the three-and-a-half-mile hike out to Dewey Point. It is one of many points overlooking Yosemite

Valley. The point provides a picturesque view of El Capitan, Bridalveil Falls, Yosemite Falls and of course, Half Dome. Unfortunately, the only view provided that day was…. gray. Cloudy gray.

We set out early Saturday morning with our day packs, our rented snowshoes in the back of the truck and no tire chains. As we were heading into the National Park, we could see that snow could be an issue. Although the roads were relatively clear, thanks to snow plows, the surrounding woods were covered in feet of snow. We exited Wawona Road onto Glacier Point Road and pulled into the parking lot of Badger Pass, a ski slope in Yosemite. The trailhead was a couple miles up the road but the plows only cleared the road to the ski slope and after our experience last winter in Kings Canyon, I wasn't going to try my luck with my toy truck and no tire chains. We would have to hike to the trailhead.

Snow levels were as high as seven feet that day and it was impossible to know where the road began and the woods ended. Luckily, vehicles with chains had driven up Glacier Point Road so we just needed to stay in their tracks until we reached the trailhead; that is, if we could find the trail marker. All the trail markers were buried under snow. Even the roadside out-houses were buried under the white stuff. Only the roofs protruded. When we noticed a trail marker nailed two feet above the snow level, we would stop and brush away the powder so we could read the sign. After clearing a half dozen signs or so, we cleared the one we were looking for; Dewey Point 3.5 miles. We strapped on our snowshoes, jumped into the snow and immediately sank to our crotches. Wings? Who needs snowshoe wings?

As with Mount San Jacinto, we were first on the trail. Any day in the spring, summer, and fall, we would want to be first on the trail. One of the main reasons we backpack and hike is to get away from people. So being first on the trail generally means that we won't run into others. In the winter, however, when there is over seven feet of fresh snow on the ground, you may not want to be first.

Once again, just like San Jacinto, the two schmucks, had to cut the trail to Dewey Point. Luckily, the landscape between Glacier Point Road and Dewey Point is relatively level so the hike wasn't near as exhausting but there was still plenty of face-planting and snowshoe-leapfrogging.

Cutting trail to Dewey Point

Although plowing through the snow to Dewey Point was exhausting, the scenery and the solitude were breathtaking. Everything was pristine white. All the trees were draped in newly fallen snow. There were no harsh winds and the temperature wasn't a factor since we were generating about 14,000 BTUs. Multiple times, in fact, each time we stopped to switch places, James and I would just admire the beauty, the tranquility, and silence surrounding us.

Besides the solitude and beauty, the hike to Dewey Point was worthwhile because it was hard and many times in life, the hard is what makes something worth doing. On the other hand, when someone else takes credit for our hard work then there could be a problem.

Once we reached Dewey Point, disappointed in the view as it was socked in by gray clouds and fog, we found a nice location under a tree, behind some rocks to cool off and have some lunch. As we sat there, congratulating each other on a job well done; and a hard job at that, a couple, male and female, of cross-country skiers arrived at the point. We could hear them talking about the lack of a view and how they were happy that someone had already cut in a trail. They obviously did not see us but we accepted their thanks quietly. A few moments later, another group of cross-country skiers arrived on the scene. One of the new arrivals, talking to the first couple on the scene, mentioned how nice it was to come through a cut trail to which the female replied, and I quote, "Thank you. It was hard cutting in the trail". James came unglued.

To be honest, I don't know if James reaction would be considered "unglued". I know what unglued looks like for me, but I don't have a lot of experience with the emotional rollercoaster of James so I'm not sure what he would consider unglued. Once, while hiking The Alder Creek Trail for the first time, of course, James came around a bend and was confronted with another hill. At that moment James took the Lord's name in vain, loudly. Since James is a respectful Catholic, I would say James came unglued. Using that moment as my baseline, when that woman took credit for cutting the trail to Dewey Point, James came unglued.

James jumped to his feet and shouted, "Are you fucking kidding me?!" I cannot tell you how those at the Point reacted as I was laughing hysterically. Once again, James provided the comedy relief that is so often needed when working hard. He did not continue his diatribe though and he did not confront the thief of our hard work. He shouted out his indignation, sat back down and we continued our ongoing conversation regarding the inevitable end of society; as supported by a person's need to take credit where none is warranted.

Dewey Point was getting crowded, in more ways than one, so we finished up lunch, packed up our gear and headed back to Glacier Point Road, our truck and the pizza and Mountain Dew waiting for us in Oakhurst.

On the way to Oakhurst, we discussed the Whitney lottery. We would provide three date options, the second weekend of August, the first weekend of August and the third weekend of August, in that order. We wanted long days as we knew it might take us over twenty hours to hike up and down (22 miles round trip at 1 mph). We wanted to be sure of the weather, so June and July were too risky. I would fill out and submit the necessary paperwork online. If we had our wish, seven months from cutting in the trail to Dewey Point, James and I would hike Mount Whitney.

The Last Trip

Although we had six months before our Whitney summit bid and six more backpacking opportunities, we only made one backpacking trip: Sphinx Creek Camp.

Sphinx Creek Camp is not on any trail guide. It's an area along Sphinx Creek where James and I dropped our packs and took a twelve-hour nap. We've reached the point in our backpacking career where we spent more time napping and wondering than actually backpacking. We were covering 2 and 3 miles per hour and reaching our campsites before noon. Backpacking was less than a struggle and more of an excuse to get away from society and contemplate our careers, our relationships, our existence. Don't get me wrong though; there were still struggles. On this trip, the struggle was reaching the top of the ridge.

For this trip, we left one Saturday morning in June with no real destination in mind. I don't recall the trail, don't remember how we got there and don't even know which park the creek lies within. I just remember a level hike; more like a walk, through a sunlit meadow. Hills, not quite mountains, lined both sides of the meadow. Further in, a river ran quickly over rocks and fallen trees. James did not have to worry about getting wet when the trail intersected the river because a beautiful wooden bridge spanned the running waters. In many places, the trail was wide enough for a small vehicle, perhaps a quad. I can imagine people driving out from the parking lot to the river and jumping in, letting the coolness of the water wash away the heat of the day and the exhaustion of life. Most people, especially those on quads, probably did not venture much further than the river and the bridge that crossed it; for once on the other side, the trail narrowed and met the base of a hill; not quite a mountain.

We stood at the base of the hill, the end of the trail, wondering what to do next. The trail appeared to end not three miles from the parking lot. There were no campsites and no left or right forks. There was, however, what appeared to be, a small trail going up (of course, up).

I would guess that the hill before us rose some 3,000 feet. I realize that most people are lousy at guessing distances, especially when looking up or down, and I may be no different. However, I have stood at the base of El Capitan and Yosemite Falls many time and I know those heights are 3400 and 3600 feet. The hill before us was all that. James and I decided it was a mountain.

With an of-course-we're-going-up laugh shared between us, we hit the switchbacks. One switchback after another; twenty feet vertically, three feet horizontally. That was the math to the top of the little-more-than a hill, little-less-than a mountain. (For the smart asses doing the math, that would equal 1,000 switchbacks and of course there were not that many. But to my lungs, heart, and mind, that math is correct) Up and up we went; twenty feet east, three feet north, twenty feet west, three feet north, until we crested the ridge. Although we stopped multiple times, we both knew that had we taken this hike years earlier, we would have run out of strength, will-power, and daylight. But today, we made the ridge before lunch and headed off into the woods.

What may or may not be Sphinx Creek

After a couple miles we ran into what we believed to be Sphinx Creek, our best guess based on a guidebook. The creek was swelled to the point of being a stream and moving briskly. It was June so the water was cold from snow in the higher elevations. We were hot from the climb so the creek provided a perfect opportunity. We kicked off our shoes, found a solid bank, and cooled with our feet hanging in the sub-50 waters. That's when it happened. The nap.

James is a nap person. He often speaks of the virtue of a Saturday afternoon nap. Laying on the couch in the middle of the day. Recharging his batteries so he can get a good night sleep eight hours later. Ignoring all the chores that lay before a grown man with a child. James is a rebel. I, on the other hand, don't like naps. I never feel better after a nap. There are things to do, like the aforementioned chores. I have no problem sleeping at night because most chores must be done in daylight. But naps cut into my get-things-done time, and I can't have that. On that day though, nothing needed to get done. We were far enough in the woods to escape society. We were prepared for Whitney. We were Tom Sawyer and Huck Finn and it was time to nap. We hastily set up out tents with every intention of waking up, gathering fire wood, having dinner, and commencing on one of our epic discussions.

Twelve hours later, aka the next morning, we awoke with the sun on the edge of the horizon; just enough light to gather wood and build a fire. We had breakfast with a couple of other hikers who made camp near our spot sometimes during our nap, broke camp and hiked out that morning.

We were no longer nervous about hiking Whitney. We were confident but not overconfident. We assumed a pace of 1 mph up and down; so we were going to leave early in the morning, in the dark so we could make it most of the way down before darkness covered the trail again. We knew what gear we needed and we had the shoes.

We knew our next hike was up Mount Whitney and we were mentally, physically, technically and spiritually prepared. We were still two schmucks, but we were two schmucks that new well what lay before them.

.

Mount Whitney

The Lottery

In February, a month after snowshoeing to Dewey Point and four months before napping along Sphinx Creek, James and I entered the Mount Whitney lottery. One-hundred hikers a day are allowed on Whitney, from the east side. If you take into account the "safe" days to hike Whitney, July through September, that's roughly ninety days or 9000 hikers allowed on Whitney. Approximately 12,000 people each year enter the Whitney lottery and approximately 40% of those are awarded a date of their choice. We were part of that 40%; karma for all our trials, for destroying the witches, for at least trying to solve the unsolvable problems, for persevering, for overcoming, for facing our shortcomings, and reaching further than we thought possible.

During the first week of April, I accepted and paid for our reservation. Two weeks later we received our passes to hike up and down Mount Whitney, in one day, on August 10, 2010. That day couldn't come soon enough.

We Ascend

After three years of backpacking and three years of planning, our big day arrived. The day we were going to hike Mount Whitney. We started out planning to backpack to the top but somewhere along the way, we decided to do Whitney in one day, one hike, 22 miles round trip. Schmucks.

Hiking Mount Whitney from the east side of the Sierra Nevadas starts at the Whitney Portal outside of Lone Pine. The portal is a drive-in campground and sits at 8,300 feet.

We were going to start the hike at 2 am on Saturday, August 10th so we met at the Whitney Portal on Friday, August 9th, James from Apple Valley in Southern California and me from Fresno in the Central Valley. I took the fork-in-the-eye route, up 395. It was as excruciating as I thought it would be; flat road, no curves, no scenery, just desert, and asphalt. The forks were so deep I now have brain damage. James arrived at the portal a couple hours before me and had already set-up camp. He also took 395 north through Trona and also had a bad case of fork-eye. James brought a full-size tent and a blow-up mattress. I brought firewood. After a hearty dinner of Dinty-Moore, we did a final check of our gear and built a fire; but, didn't stay up long. Man, 2 a.m. comes early.

We left camp as planned, at 2 a.m. That's 2 o'clock in the morning. 0200 military. Zero-dark-hundred. It was August and it was dark. It was brisk, but not cold. We knew coats would not be needed as experience taught us that hiking up-hill quickly provides all the warmth needed on brisk, and sometimes even cold mornings. Dark on the other hand is something different. No matter how steep the climb, or how much you sweat, you cannot generate light. Light is something that must be provided from outside your body and that morning light came in the form of headlamps (often called "geek-lights").

The first time James strapped on his headlamp, some 36 months earlier, I made fun of him. He reminded me of Rick Moranis in the movie "Honey I Shrunk the Kids". Not that James looks like Rick Moranis, but he definitely had that nerdy scientist vibe about him with the headlamp, and its harness, firmly strapped over his head. Hence the name "geek-light." Of course, that morning, at 2 a.m., there were two nerdy scientist types hiking through the woods of Mount Whitney.

With Montrail shoes, nylon convertible pants, backpacks riding on our hips filled with food, space blankets, and headlamps firmly strapped on our heads, we hit the trail to the top of Mount Whitney. I couldn't stop smiling and although it was dark, I knew James was smiling as well. The time had finally arrived. After nearly 36 months of backpacking, we were finally on the Whitney Trail. After the failure at Alder Creek and the dominance of Alder Creek, we were moving up to the summit. All of our failures were behind us. Lessons learned in our minds. All of our successes would pale in comparison if the day went as planned. This was the day that we proved to ourselves that we could still be "men", still meet the challenge, still, dig a little deeper for the strength to move forward. This was our crab boat, our call to the wild, our I-can-top-that-story moment and we were finally on the trail.

As the sun climbed over the horizon and the headlamps came off, a rock slide came into view. The rock slide did not cross the trail so no spider crawl was necessary. The slide was to our left. It appeared that years ago a fire ravaged the side of the mountain and erosion had stripped away the remaining vegetation. Since then, the area had become a gathering place of stones and small boulders. Luckily the trail avoided the area altogether and started downward. Even on Mount Whitney, the Fundamental Law of Backpacking applies. We had been hiking up all morning and now we're on our way down, but clearly, we needed to go back up. The trail leveled off in a lush, green meadow crossed by a mid-size stream. Luckily for James, someone had built a bridge over the stream. At the far end of the meadow, off the trail, a small waterfall, some 12 feet high, kept the stream filled and flowing. After crossing the meadow, the trail resumed its uphill climb. (Fundamental Law in action)

When starting the hike, I didn't really notice the grade of the ascent. I believe vision can affect physical abilities as much as muscles. When faced with a vertical assault, like climbing to the top of Yosemite Falls, the site of the climb impacts your muscle's ability to execute. It's why to get the best out of someone, you may need to blindfold them so their mind doesn't give up before their muscles. When we began the day it was dark and the headlamps didn't throw light far enough forward to give an impression of the climb before us. Sometimes, we would turn off the headlamps and walk in the dark. Until of course, our imagination got the best of us and we needed light to ward off the wolves, zombies, wendigos, and anything else that lurks in the minds of those wishing for the end of the world. Without the benefit of light, our eyes couldn't tell us that the climb was too steep; James and I just walked and talked, letting our muscles and the moonlight lead the way. Now, however, with the sun lighting the meadow, we could see the climb on the other side of the meadow. Our eyes began to raise doubts.

But we were good. Our packs did not weigh 35 pounds and we were not the same two people that doubled-over trying to reach the summit of Alta Peak. We left the meadow and started the switchbacks that would take us to the backpacker's campsite.

The backpacker's campsite is located at 12,000 feet above sea level. Calling it a campsite is a stretch. It is an area roughly measuring 2000 square feet, according to my blurry estimates, and there are no trees, no vegetation, no wood, just small rocks, and dirt. Single man tents, sleeping bags, and bivy sacks were strewn about the place. Zombies with bed-head meandered to and fro. It looked like the day after Woodstock or the day before Burning Man or the day after my annual Christmas Party. In other words, it didn't look good and James and I were glad we decided to complete Whitney in one day. After crossing through the dead zone, the hike up begins in earnest.

At this point, since you're well above 10,000 feet, all manner of greenery is gone. There is only stone, rock, and gravel. Hard edges everywhere you looked. To clarify, gravel is small hard shit that works its way into your shoes and makes it uncomfortable to walk. Rock is large hard shit that is under your shoes and causes you to twist your ankle our gives way and causes you to slide back, giving up all progress and stone is what the trail was cut into. Stone is also what was used to secure the "railings", and I use the term railings loosely.

After you cross the backpacker's camp, the trail narrows and ascends on the front side, the east side, of Mount Whitney. During this part of the hike, the only thing stopping someone from falling from the trail and landing some 3,000 feet below is their mountain goat like balance and a makeshift railing of spikes and cables. Spikes have been driven into the stone of the mountain and cables were looped from spike to spike. Although the cables are certainly strong enough to support a person, there is nothing above or below the cable. If someone were to fall, with any kind of force, into the cable, they would pinwheel around the cable and then fall to their certain death. Obviously, the cables are there to provide a handhold to steady one's self, not to prevent a most painful plunge. James did not like this part of the trail and although I'm more secure with heights, my ass was puckering as we maneuvered through this narrow stretch.

On the backside of the mountain, the west side, there was no rail. You would still probably die if you fell off the backside, but you wouldn't plunge to your death. You would roll, tumble, slide and bounce to your death, because the backside is more sloped, so you wouldn't plunge, per se. You'd simply be ground into taco meat by the aforementioned hard shit. Clearly the backside didn't need a rail. The backside didn't have something else the front side had, a trail; which was kind of important since we had planned to hike to the summit on an actual trail. To be honest, there was a trail, but since it was covered in constantly falling gravel and rock, the trail was all but invisible. If you kept your eyes down and focused on the three feet of gravel in front of you, you could see the trail. If you looked up, however, the trail would disappear. Considering James' acrophobia, keeping his eyes down and focused on the three feet in front of him, was not a problem and he led the way through this portion of the hike.

The trail appears and reappears for about a mile and then begins climbing in earnest, straight through a field of gravel and scree. We were on the final push to the summit. We could hear hikers in the distance. We could see the stone shelter that was erected years ago on the summit. We were close. We knew we would make it. As our anticipation grew, our strength grew, our determination grew. After the assault on Alta Peak, we knew we had this and fifteen minutes later, James and I were standing on the summit of Mount Whitney. What started out 36 months and nine hours ago as a conversation culminated in two schmucks sitting atop the highest point in the contiguous United States.

Just like all the hikers on the summit that day, James and I congratulated each other. We gave each other high fives. We sat at the highest point and took pictures. We walked through the stone shelter. We shared stories with other hikers. We signed the Whitney Guest Book and perused all of the other names of those that came before us and those who were there with us. We had lunch. We were stalling. At some point, we had to go down.

We Descend

Descending Whitney was like ending a long journey. Our spirits were high and our steps were light. We had planned. We had trained. We had achieved. We were going home the victors. James and I walked and talked through the amazing disappearing trail. We laughed and hopped down the front side of the mountain, barely grasping the spike and cable railing. We sauntered through the dead zone. We began slowing down as we entered the meadow. We were getting gassed I was dragging when we reached the rock slide. Whitney wasn't done with us. Not yet. I lost all hope forty minutes later when Mathilda passed us.

I first met Mathilda (a name I assigned) on the summit. Mathilda was 85 years old, gray-haired, 5' 3" Grandmother. And Mathilda was on the summit with us. Mathilda left the summit before we did and we caught up with her in the meadow where she was resting against a log fence. We waved and told her we would see her at the bottom. Forty minutes later Mathilda waved as she passed us and we did not see her again.

Three years of training and all we accomplished was hiking to the top of Mount Whitney, and down, slower than an 85-year-old Grandmother. We are schmucks.

No matter though, we accomplished our goal. We were manly men, dammit! So, I pulled it back together, summoned the strength I would need to finish, and with Mathilda pulling away, and we resumed our descent. Forty minutes later I told James to go on without me.

I blame it on my eyes. As explained earlier, your eyes can sap the strength from your muscles and by now we could see the parking lot below. Problem was, the parking lot wasn't getting any closer. We were hiking on switchbacks and the descent was so gradual that a thousand feet of hiking resulted in only 100 feet of descent. Maybe 100. It felt like 25. James has this cool watch with an altimeter built in so, we always know where we are based on altitude and time. After countless times of me asking about the elevation, James had begun to lie to me because he didn't have the heart to tell me the truth. He knew my psyche couldn't take the fact that we weren't going down, just vertically back and forth, so he always tacked on an extra 50 feet of descent to keep me motivated. My eyes were cruel to me that day.

A family of four passed by. It was embarrassing. I was moving again.

What started as high spirits and light steps ended as a death march.

Of course, no one died that day. In time, a lot of time, and more than a few expletives regarding the glacial pace of our descent, we made the Whitney Portal and our campsite; sixteen hours later. A little more than a mile an hour. Hot Damn!

To the Victor Goes the Prize

On that summer's day in 2007, we sat on Garfield Peak in Crater Lake National Park and decided to take on backpacking. We took on the weather and the witches and our own stupidity. We camped along a stream in Los Padres and decided to take on Whitney. We took on snow and altitude and our own stupidity. We took on bears and darkness and of course, our own stupidity. And in the end, we won every battle. Not because we were able to hike to the top of Whitney, but because we kept going. We kept returning to the wilderness to challenge ourselves because we had more to give. Although Whitney was the goal, it wasn't the prize. The prize was the time James and I spent in the wilderness learning about ourselves and building a bond that cannot be severed by witches, weather, bears, darkness, snow, altitude or, ……our own stupidity.

Made in the USA
Columbia, SC
28 November 2022